"They have sought Thee at many altars,
they have carried lights to find Thee;
I find Thee in the white fire of my heart."

White Fire

White Fire

THE LIFE AND WORKS

of

JESSIE SAMPTER

BY

BERTHA BADT-STRAUSS

THE RECONSTRUCTIONIST PRESS

New York • *1956*

DESIGNED BY HARVEY SATENSTEIN
MANUFACTURED IN THE UNITED STATES OF AMERICA BY
BOOK CRAFTSMEN ASSOCIATES, INC., NEW YORK

To the memory of Milton Steinberg,
who, like Jessie Sampter,
was a lover of the People and the Land of Israel
and a stalwart advocate
of social justice for all mankind.

Foreword

The opinion is widely prevalent that, while American Jewry has made notable financial contributions to the development of the land of Israel and has been helpful, politically, to the State of Israel, it has contributed little to the spiritual development of the new nation. That impression is a result, no doubt, of the small number of American Jews who have gone to Israel to participate in its development. The truth is, however, that though American settlers in Israel have been few in number, among those who have settled in that country have been distinguished personalities who have set high sights for its spiritual objectives, such personalities as Judah L. Magnes, Henrietta Szold and the subject of this biography, Jessie Sampter.

The title, "White Fire," taken from one of her poems, is an apt term to describe the ardor of Miss Sampter's passionate and pure devotion to the realization of her ideals. She was not a sentimentalist, to whom the mere emotional response to ideals was sufficient, but a practical person, who was always looking for opportunities to participate personally in their achievement. That spirit sent her on a long quest. Her goals kept changing; never arbitrarily, but always as a logical consequence of her earlier insights. Reared in a family which was steeped in American culture but had largely severed its connection with Jewish tradition, she responded intensely to the "ethical culture" in which she grew up. But her poetic soul could not long be at rest in such a deracinated, abstract culture and ethics. She longed for religion and found it in the Jewish tradition. However, a formalistic religion no more satisfied her spiritual yearnings than did universal ethics, and she sought a combination of the two by dedication to a live movement which did not merely pay ritual tribute to ethical social ideals, but also gave creative expression to them. Such a movement she found in Zionism, and particularly in that branch of Zionism which was most creative, in Labor Zionism, which endeavored, by the application of work on the land and the establishment of cooperative institutions, to effect an ethical social order in keeping with the highest religious ideals. Spurning mere verbal expression of her interest in Zion, she settled in Israel and shared in the hardships of a pioneering life in a country that was still mostly desert.

That alone would have been an achievement worthy of recording for generations to come. What made it even more notable, however, was that it was accomplished under the handicap of physical illness and torment. As a child, Jessie Sampter had suffered from an attack of poliomyelitis which left her feeble and deformed. But she would not let her physical weaknesses interfere with her life's purpose. Though she could not engage in hard manual work, she shared in the self-denial demanded of the *halutz* and became the poet of *halutziut*.

Dr. Bertha Badt-Strauss, her biographer, understood her. Wisely keeping herself in the background, Dr. Badt-Strauss tells the story of Jessie's life, principally in her heroine's own words. Quotations from her diaries, her letters and her writings, show how intimately her poetry expressed her life, and how her life embodied her poetic and religious soul.

It is well that this book makes its appearance at the present time. Disillusionment and cynicism, in many circles of the Jewish as well as of the general world, have effaced the idealism of the days when Zionism was still mainly a dream. Compromises have been made and disappointments have been experienced. We have need, therefore, of the message of encouragement that flows from the life of Jessie Sampter. Neither disappointment nor physical pain could destroy her faith in her ideals or deter her from pursuing them. The message of her writings and the inspiration of her example are more needed now than even in her lifetime.

Jewish life today is in need of reconstruction, of a reconstruction that proceeds from a rededication to the highest ideals of the Jewish tradition. That is why the Reconstructionist Press feels it a privilege and an honor to publish this book. We are profoundly indebted to its author for giving us the opportunity to do so. If "the memory of the righteous is a blessing," those who save from oblivion the records of so saintly and dedicated a life as that of Jessie Sampter confer a genuine blessing on their people and make a notable contribution to the perpetuation and enrichment of the Jewish spirit.

EUGENE KOHN

Acknowledgments

I wish to record here my deep sense of obligation to all the numerous people and institutions who, by graciously answering my innumerable questions and furnishing valuable information, helped me write this book. I regret that limitations of space preclude my mentioning each and every one of them. The following, however, made outstanding contributions to the book:

First and foremost, Mrs. Edgar Wachenheim, Jessie Sampter's devoted sister, who gave me information about her life, access to her correspondence and to many of her unpublished writings.

Mrs. Virginia Liebowitz, Mr. and Mrs. Arthur Meyer, Mrs. Amy Segal, Professor Alexander Dushkin, Mr. Meyer Weisgal, Mr. Carl Alpert, and Miss Leah Berlin, all of whom sent me important letters bearing on Jessie Sampter's life.

Mr. Emil Simon, Mrs. Louis W. Rice, Professor Louis Wise, Israel Bar Shira and Miss Anda Pinkerfeld, who made available unpublished works, out of print material and other writings of Jessie Sampter not easily available in this country.

Mrs. Dorothy Alofsin, who first called the attention of American Jewish youth to the memory of Jessie Sampter, and who also wrote me an informative letter about her.

Mr. Hyman Segal, who sent me an eloquent pen-picture of his first meeting with her.

Dr. Mordecai M. Kaplan, who let me see the protocols of the Sabbath afternoon discussion group which Jessie Sampter attended at his home.

Dr. Eugene Kohn who carefully edited my manuscript and helped me by many valuable suggestions, and Mrs. Elsie Farrow who typed the manuscript.

Moreover, the Hebrew Union College Library in Cincinnati and the Jewish Theological Seminary in New York supplied me with many of Jessie Sampter's books which had long been out of print. Without the courteous assistance of the staffs of these libraries and that of Miss Mary Frances Smith, the librarian of Centenary College, Shreveport, this book could never have been written.

Also, the Administration of Givat Brenner in Israel sent me Jessie's last picture, the copy of a charcoal drawing by Muriel Bentwich, the Hebrew memorial book, *Yesha*, and many informative letters.

Finally I should like to thank the two men in my immediate family, my husband, Professor Bruno Strauss of Centenary College and my son, Albrecht B. Strauss of Yale University, for their unwavering interest and patience. Both read my manuscript and made many helpful suggestions.

B. B-S.

List of Illustrations

Contents

White Fire

Childhood in the Sampter Mansion

But what will be the life of the limping
young girl? . . .
. . . Will her lips
grow pursed by bitterness of deprivation?
Will she lie awake envious at night?
In daytime will her wish deceive her,
make her well?
Or: will she overcome her handicap?
For this small grievous difference
will grow up with her, will at every step
silently lead her aside from the crowd
will daily make her suffer it anew. . . .
Cannot destroy her; only lead her on.
She is so light; if far enough it leads,
she will Eternity and all it means
more quickly grasp than all her girlish
friends, and blessed every morning she
will come
Back from her stars, wearing her wings
inside. . . .
R. M. Rilke, *Gedichte aus dem Nachlass*
(Translated by B. B-S.).

A little girl, pale and delicate and about five years old, was running round and round the table in the big play room in the Sampter Mansion on Fifth Avenue in New York . . . running and running, and weeping silently and abundantly. Anxiously her fragile mother asked: "Why do you cry, Jessie dear? What ails you, darling? What is the matter with you?"

"Oh, nothing at all, Mamma!" replied the child. "But I've been telling myself such a sad story!"

That was the beginning of Jessie Sampter's literary career. As a matter of fact, the child started to compose her rhymes and stories before she knew how to read and write. Her devoted mother listened to her and jotted down what she heard the child chanting to herself.

At that time—Jessie Ethel Sampter was born on March 22nd, 1883 — the Sampters lived a life of ease and plenty in their big family house, which Grandpa Sampter had built on Fifth Avenue in Harlem in 1880. But the Sampters had not always lived that way. Michael Sampter had been a grain merchant in Eastern Germany near the Polish border in the small town of Samter. One day, the Mayor of the town declined to renew his license for selling grain. Michael came home and told his clever wife, Rachel, about it. To his surprise, she did not seem upset by the news. "All right!" she replied. "Here are my four little boys. I never wanted to see them grow up to be soldiers in this country. You go ahead to America; I shall stay here and run your household in the meantime, and wait till you send for us!"

A family tradition knew the reason of this valiant answer of Rachel's. Raised as one of the daughters of a wealthy landowner, she had seen her parents' estate looted by soldiers in war-time. She never forgot how she and her pretty sisters had had to hide in the cellar and blacken their faces in order to avoid the soldiers' assaults. So, a pacifist by her own bitter experience, she hated every soldier, and when the universal draft had become law in Germany, she was more than willing to leave that country.

Grandpa Sampter did what his clever wife wanted him to do and emigrated to America. As a newcomer, he was glad to find a poorly paid job in a tailor shop in New York. But this was the decade of the successful immigrant from Europe; soon he learned the trade and bought his own shop. It was then that he sent for Rachel and the boys. These were difficult years for the little family. Later on, Rachel often used to tell her grandchildren how she had had to help her husband all she could in those beginnings in America. Often, so she said, when her babies were but a few days old, she would sit up in her bed and sew buttons on the suits that were manufactured in the Sampter factory. At her suggestion, they were the first to sell ready-made boys' clothes, so that the mammas did not have to sew their boys' pants as they had done before. The Sampter business grew and grew until it represented one of the largest wholesale men's clothing concerns in New York. Mother Rachel, "the Boss," as her daughters-in-law called her, was consulted every night at every new step in business.

More children were born in New York to the Michael Sampters: two boys and a girl, Jenny. The six boys all attended public schools. Rudolph, the eldest, Jessie's father, had, from his earliest youth, nourished the wish to become a lawyer. The gifted boy finished school at the age of twelve and took all sorts of odd jobs; he went to night school and finally got his degree from Columbia University. Otto, Arnold and Morris helped in the store; another son, Emile, died of tuberculosis, when he was only nineteen.

Meanwhile, young Rudolph had fallen in love with Virginia Kohlberg, whose father, Jacob Kohlberg, had also come from Germany. This adventurous man had come on a sailing vessel around Cape Horn to find gold, as did many people, in the years of the "Gold Rush." After he had succeeded in getting to America, Jacob's next thought was to find a wife and build up a family. He learned that the Rosenbaums had come over from his own home town, Beverungen near Cassel, so he took a trip back east and returned with his bride, Edel Rosenbaum. Edel had never seen her prospective bridegroom before, but she was willing to marry him, became his devoted wife and bore him nine children. With all her household duties, Grandma Edel was well read and romantically inclined. She called her first son Manfred after Lord Byron's hero, and her first daughter was called Virginia after a favorite love story of that time, "Paul and Virginia." It is strange, but typical of the attitude of the Western towards the Eastern Jew that, at first, the Kohlbergs strongly objected to Virginia's marriage to Rudolph because the Sampters came from the East, and so were "Pollacks."

Moved by a sort of homesickness not infrequent in those decades, the Kohlbergs had gone back to Germany when little Virginia was two years old; but seven years later they returned to America to stay there. Grandpa Kohlberg had invested part of his money and lost it, but now he had learned his lesson; he settled in New York, started a successful tobacco business and raised his nine children in ease and comfort. The Kohlbergs never were as successful businessmen as the Sampters, but their adventurous spirit inspired the imagination of young Jessie and lived on in her poetry:

"My people is a bold adventurous people,
My great-grandfather fought Napoleon
And lost his sight — he did not lose his vision.
And my grandfather sailed a merchant-man
Around two continents to a wild coast
Among wild men and mountains to dig gold
And spent the gold he toiled for, and died poor."

The little girl in the big Sampter house on Fifth Avenue in Harlem never was lonely; cousins and grandparents, uncles and aunts lived in all the different stories of the family house. The Sampter grandparents lived on the first floor; Rudolph, the eldest son and his little family — his wife Virginia and his two little girls, Elvie and Jessie — occupied three rooms on the second floor. Above them lived the Otto Sampters with their

"The Old House," 2138 - 5th Ave., New York, N. Y.

family, the twins Edith and Aimee and their two brothers. A spacious kitchen and pantry furnished the elegant dinners served in the big dining-room for all the members of the "clan."

This house seems to have been a typical house of the successful immigrant in the last decades of the 19th century. It played an important role in the youthful life of Jessie Sampter, and so we welcome the chance to get better acquainted with it by means of an unpublished autiobiographical novel of Jessie Sampter's which she called *Hester Lynn*.

The "Old House" was loved by all the children of the family and sadly missed, when Grandpa Michael was compelled to part with it, after the Sampter factory no longer flourished as before. It was built in the flamboyant style of the last century, decorated with crystal chandeliers and large frescoes on walls and ceilings; wide kitchens and pantries were in the basement, and in the garden were stables and living quarters for the coachman and his family. Grandma Rachel, who changed her first name to "Rose" in later years, liked to drive through Central Park in the afternoons in her victoria. Usually, one of the grandchildren was expected to accompany her. The children hated it; but their little friends from across the street were full of envy.

In Jessie Sampter's novel we see the "Old House" in all its glory, surrounded by green meadows which gradually had to give place to new houses. For, as the children grew up, New York grew up with them. Still, the magnificent garden remained, this "wonderland of games" as the novel calls it. More than twenty rosebushes gave their fragrance in summer, and the neighborhood children often came to the wooden fence to ask for flowers. The enormous horse-chestnut tree, with its luscious clusters of blossoms and its wide, hanging branches, which in June almost formed a sort of tent, was never forgotten by Jessie. Even in the eucalyptus groves of Palestine she longed for this bower of her childhood. No wonder she did not forget it; it was the favorite meeting place of the two "chums" of the house, Jessie herself, and her cousin Ethel. Here most of the stories were told, by means of which Jessie, the born story-teller, enchanted a willing audience of cousins and friends. When April showers came down, the children used to escape into the latticed summer house, a pleasant refuge for all the youngsters of the family.

In summer, Father Rudolph and his little family set out for "Sylvan Camp," at Long Lake in the Adirondacks, a rustic property far away from the town. There the two girls, sturdy tomboyish Elvie and pale delicate Jessie, lived an outdoor life, clad in bloomers and protected from the sun by big red felt hats. Perhaps this is where Jessie first tasted the joys of pioneer life which she was to experience later on in Palestine. To be sure, the Sampters were far from lonely in their summer camp. They brought servants and even a governess along with them; and what is more, each summer, as soon as their father's young lawyer friends knew that they had left for the Camp, they never hesitated to take advantage of the pleasant and well-known Sampter hospitality. The children listened to many interesting discussions and were expected to speak up just like the adults.

Taken all in all, life in the Sampter Mansion was a "Contented Life," as Van Wyck Brooks called this whole era in American history. The Sampters certainly knew how to enjoy their hard-earned wealth; but withal they were generous enough, and Michael Sampter helped many a needy nephew or niece to come to America. The newcomers were given jobs in his factory and stayed at the "mansion," until they had their own homes. Grandma Rachel, in the meantime, looked around for wives for the nephews and husbands for the nieces so that the family might prosper and multiply.

However, not all the summers were given to this pleasant life in their Sylvan Camp. Once, the whole family went to

Europe to consult physicians for Rudolph, who was thought to have the lung disease which had killed his young brother. For the time being, this trip to Meran, to Montreux, to Reichenhall was an exciting adventure for the children. Mother Virginia always hired servants and a governess in these resort places so that their education might not be interrupted. One of these governesses, a big German woman from Leipzig, is said to have spoiled Jessie and unjustly punished her older sister Elvie, a proceeding which pained both the girls, Elvie because she felt mistreated and Jessie, because she abhorred injustice.

THE ETHICAL CULTURE BACKGROUND

Rudolph Sampter seems to have been the hero of Jessie's childhood dreams. Though she adored mother and sister, she confessed in her novel "to have loved him just a little more, because he understood." Often, when the nervous, highstrung child awoke screaming at night, Father Rudolph would get up, light the candle and carry her around to show her that there were no ghosts or hobgoblins in the room, nothing to fear, absolutely nothing. Moreover, this father understood Jessie's special gift for poetry. He used to read and criticize her poems; sometimes, when he liked a poem, he had it bound in cardboard to preserve it; but on the other hand, when a poem seemed to him over-sentimental, he read it out to the young author and stressed the comic effects. In the end, both author and critic had to laugh, "for he had the saving graces of a genial sense of humor and a deep love of life," as Jessie summed it up in her novel.

This brilliant man was an avowed atheist all the days of his life. In his leisure hours he read Darwin and Ingersoll, and he was proud to be a friend and disciple of Felix Adler the apostle of Ethical Culture. Like the majority of his fellow immigrants in those decades, he had discarded the traditions and customs of his Jewish faith; in his house, Hanukkah and Passover had been obliterated by Christmas and Easter eggs, as his daughter Jessie wrote in her "Confession" in later years. Only one tenet of Judaism remained as basis of his educational efforts: the love of truth. "Tell the truth and never be afraid!" These were the laws which reigned in Jessie Sampter's childhood; she never forgot them in all her life. In fact, they served as a torch to show her the way to her ancient faith. "Mamma, am I Jewish?" asked the little girl, when she was about eight years old, running in from the street. "Why yes, Jessie, why do you ask?" replied her mother. "Because I told the children that I am NOT! I better run out right now and tell them that I am, or they will think I told them a lie!"

This little true story does more than any lengthy discussion to characterize the educational life of the Sampter household. It is true that Mother Virginia, coming from a traditional Jewish home, made her little girls recite a short German prayer before going to sleep at night; but this shadowy God of early childhood seems to have faded away when the girls grew up and tragedy came into their life. It is most significant that Jessie, the fanatic of truth, completely forgot in later years to mention these early night prayers in her "Confession" and repeatedly called her home a "godless household." She must have felt that she had lost this childhood God early in life and never really addressed her prayers to Him. There was a time in her life when Jessie considered the absence of any fixed religion in her father's house a definite asset. But as a teen-ager, she seems to have bitterly missed a God to whom she could pray; longingly, she looked at the servants who were the only persons who did pray in the Sampter house.

In all other respects, the two little girls received a most careful, though decidedly "Victorian," education. Nobody bothered to tell them about the facts of life; the baby in George

Eliot's "Adam Bede" puzzled them by its unknown origin. Language training they got from their mother, who had attended school in Hanover, and always spoke German to the girls, and, in later years, from a young French girl who lived with them, adding French to the curriculum. Elvie and all the other Sampter cousins attended public schools, but Jessie was taught at home, because her father thought her too sickly and delicate to bear the strain of school life. One of her early poems, "My School," which appeared in the *St. Nicholas Magazine,* reveals that this measure of care caused much heartbreak to the lonely child who had to stay at home when the others trudged away to school in the mornings and came back in the afternoon, ruddy-faced and boisterous. The little philosopher somewhat precociously comforted herself by turning to the wisdom of the "woods and glen" with "smiles to keep the tears away":

"Ah, you have bonny things to tell of school days
    long gone by
Your cheeks were ruddy as you went, your hearts
    were light — but I
I watched you caper down the road to
    knowledgeland — and then
With smiles to keep the tears away, I wandered
    toward the glen,
The woods, the rills, the haunted nooks, where
    many an imp and elf
Was waiting for the sickly child, my poor
    untutored self. . . ."

THE DEATH OF JESSIE'S FATHER AND HER ILLNESS

All this carefree and happy life came to an end when Father Rudolph, though not more than forty-five years old, died of

pneumonia in 1895.* His fine, sensitive wife never fully regained her former peace of mind. She continued to wear the
garments of mourning for a long time, and the shadow of be-
reavement did not vanish from the home. In the same year,
another disaster struck the little family. In the fall, their much
admired and petted "problem child" Jessie, who at this time
was thirteen years old, was stricken by a dire disease. They
called it "brain-fever" at that time; it would have been called
"polio" today. The little girl had to stay in bed for months,
and, afterwards, when she was allowed to get up, her fingers
remained wasted and weak and her spine developed a curvature, which had to be corrected by a heavy brace. What is more,
she had to give up her fondest dream. Jessie had planned to
become a violinist; her teacher had praised her gift and made
her hope to attain full artistic achievement. Now she had to
bury this dream; but long after she grew up, her friends saw
her violin in Jessie's room in its usual place. Did she in her
heart of hearts still hope to get completely well? She never told
anybody what was in her heart; but it is deeply moving and
tell-tale too, that years later, in *The Speaking Heart*, her unpublished autobiography, she revealed that once in her life
she had had a vision, in which she dreamed that her fingers
were strong and well again as they had been before her illness.
She was cruelly disappointed when she awoke and found them
wasted as always.

However, this illness did not break Jessie's courageous soul,
but "made her stronger." When she was still in bed, she asked
for her scissors, managed to hold them between two fingers,

---

* On Febr. 26, 1895, the New York *Times* announced Rudolph Sampter's death
in a significant note "R. S., senior member of the law firm of Sampter & Fleish-
mann of 329 Broadway, died at his home 2138 Fifth Avenue yesterday morning.
. . . Mr. Sampter was a member of the Ethical Culture Society. In the workings
of this society he took a deep interest, and as far as his health permitted, took
an active part. He was connected with no other religious body.
. . . The body will be cremated."

and cut out her silhouettes as before. All her friends knew that she sewed beautifully and knew how to turn out the most perfect "rag-dolls" for the children. In later years, she also painted in her leisure hours. On the whole, Jessie liked all kinds of "handicraft." With a sort of relish she often turned to her sewingbox, when tired of brain-work and bookish lore. As a child, she had been sweetly pretty with her corkscrew curls and big, luminous eyes. Everybody had been in the habit of spoiling and petting her, but now she objected to more spoiling and became a fighter. Sometimes she succeeded in ignoring her illness and making others forget it. Perhaps her indomitable will to go her own way in matters spiritual as well as in everyday life, enabled her in later years to become the advocate of ideas which all her family opposed; this will grew up in the days of her illness.

So, after all, the young patient was not unhappy. Her childhood gift of "make believe" had not left her, and in the midst of all her boisterous, merry playfellows, Jessie remained the favorite story-teller. She knew the secret of linking today's episode to that of tomorrow, so that the "soap-operas" of radio fame would have had nothing to teach her. It was in those years that she began to send her poems and stories to the *St. Nicholas Magazine,* just as another famous woman lyricist, Edna St. Vincent Millay, did a little later. This children's magazine appeared in those decades in every cultured household with the same regularity as did the adults' magazine. In fact, parents read it to their small children before the children themselves could read. Jessie's poems were accepted and she won various prizes and "gold badges." It was a proud day in her young life when Albert Bigelow Paine, the editor of the *St. Nicholas Magazine* and the author of the first biography of Mark Twain came to see her. He wanted, he said, to make the acquaintance of the fifteen year old girl who had sent him a thoughtful poem like "The Old Coat."* This visit was proudly described in Jessie's unpublished novel, *Hester Lynn*.

And so the tragic end of her happy childhood, Jessie's fateful illness, may have turned out to be a blessing in disguise. It did not vanquish her will-power; on the contrary, it strengthened her power to resist and enabled her to go her own way. "What does not defeat you, strengthens you!" — Only a girl who knew suffering as Jessie did was fit to become the frail woman but great educator and humanitarian whom we admire.

---

* For this and another childhood poem, see Appendix A, page 185.

II

Early Life and Poetry

> I love this fearful world. I trust the Unknown, because it is the whole of myself. The space holds me, and the darkness spreads a great light. For this is the bottomless pit and the roofless heaven and in it I AM FOREVER.
> *The Great Adventurer.*

As soon as she had sufficiently recovered her health after the attack of infantile paralysis, Jessie tried with might and main to return to all her former activities — to her sewing, to cutting out silhouettes and also to her education. In spite of all obstacles, she managed to attend courses at Columbia, and she even took a course in short story writing with Prof. Abbott in 1902/03. However, in later years she did not overestimate the value of these educational efforts. When she was a wellknown writer and was asked by the "American Who's Who" to state the education she had received, she replied "self-educated." In fact, she and her whole family seemed to prefer that sort of education. Although the Sampters were now far from affluent, Mother Virginia managed to take her two girls on extended tours all over Europe. Frequently they were joined by the Brands — Virginia's youngest sister Ottilie, her brilliant but often ailing husband, and their three young children.

So, in 1889, they went to Europe with the Brands, rented a small house in Hampstead Heath in London and took in an

English girl as a visiting governess for the children. Here they met many English poets. Jessie experienced the thrill of meeting Israel Zangwill, the author of *Children of the Ghetto*. However, this experience was a little set-back for the teen-age girl with her brown curls, which she wore shoulder-length according to the fashion of those years; the Zangwill's maid escorted Jessie to the nursery, as she thought that she was a friend of the children in the house.

Next year, the Sampters again joined the Brands in a visit to the British Isles. This time, they made a point of visiting the homes of the English poets in the Lake District and elsewhere. Long afterwards, in the orange groves of Palestine, Jessie remembered how she had recited Keats and Shelley, whose poetry she knew by heart, in a rowboat on Lake Windermere. This time, the two Sampter girls, themselves, took care of the education of the Brand children. They established school classes out in the open air on the lawn and taught their more or less willing pupils history and geography. The following year, they went to Ireland, sketched, and became interested in bird study. Jessie had first been advised to look at the birds in the trees by a doctor who was hopeful that this would help to correct the curvature of her spine, the result of her polio attack. Now she made a virtue of this necessity and studied bird nests of all kinds; she even took them home, to the digust of her family, who feared them as a breeding place for all sorts of insects.

In these years of journeying, the Sampters in no wise neglected their American heritage. In 1902, they visited the "American shrine," Concord, where Jessie's "saint," Ralph Waldo Emerson had lived and taught. They came back to this memorable place twice afterwards, as Jessie had been inspired by the atmosphere. Much to her delight, they met Emerson's sister and his grand-children, as well as a grand-daughter of Nathaniel Hawthorne.

In a later year, they again derived literary benefit from one of their summer trips. This time, they had the good luck to meet Prof. Chamberlain of Clark University in Maine. They became great friends, and Prof. Chamberlain invited Jessie, in spite of her scant schooling, to become a member of Clark University and teach psychology there. Her uncertain health wrecked this tempting plan, but through Chamberlain, who had invited Jessie to be his guest at Worcester, Jessie met the famous Harvard philosopher, Prof. Josiah Royce, who later on willingly consented to write an introduction to her strange book, *The Seekers.*

In between, they had quiet summers with Grandpa Sampter in Arverne, where Jessie wrote many youthful poems about the woods, about "Lady Moon" and "The Lake." These were admired by her many cousins, though they were little more than the conventional products of a facile versifier. However, there is one surprising poem among these "infantile outpourings," as Jessie, who always was her own severest critic, called them in later years. It is entitled "Cry unto Moses" and deals with a cruel episode in the history of the English Jews. Did Zangwill influence her to turn to this theme? Or did she study Graetz's History of the Jews? We do not know for certain. But this poem, though it is wordy and long-winded, stands like a torch in the midst of all the other innocent, average poems of the summer traveler and seems to foreshadow Jessie's future interests and her special mission.

The Meeting With Literary Friends

In the course of these years, Jessie had won the friendship of an unusual young girl whose name was destined to be well known in the world of American literature. She was Mary Antin, the author of the classical story of the Eastern-Jewish immigrant who discovered in America the real "Promised Land" of Biblical times. Mary, who was slightly older than

Jessie, had been born in Polotzk (Russia) in 1881, and Israel
Zangwill had been the first to call the attention of the literary
world to her gift. It was indeed a success, when the *Atlantic
Monthly* published her afterwards well-known story, "The
Promised Land" among its firsts.

Jessie met Mary Antin at a reception at the home of Israel
Zangwill during one of his New York visits, and soon the two
girls discovered how much they had in common. Their friendship remained steadfast through all the vicissitudes of their
lives down to the day of Jessie's death. In fact, there is a sort
of mystery about this friendship which survived all the different creeds and theories that Mary embraced in later life. It
seems as if Jessie was one of the very few persons who knew
Mary's innermost soul. In *The Speaking Heart,* Mary is described as one of the few, almost the only one, with whom
Jessie dared speak about matters of faith. Incidentally, in her
meetings in later years with Dr. Mordecai M. Kaplan, Jessie
herself stood up for her friend who had been attacked for her
attitude to Judaism. Jessie held fast to the theory that Mary
was, herself, a whole hearted Jewess who had painted the portrait of the immigrant in her *Promised Land* in an earlier
period of her life, when she had been overwhelmed by the first
impression of the new world and had been estranged from
Judaism. In the meantime, Mary had progressed to a higher
unity between Americanism and Judaism and had become
"a better American by becoming a better Jew" to use the words
of Judge Brandeis.*

---

* Mary Antin herself seems to have undergone a development similar to that
of her friend Jessie Sampter. There was a time in her life when she felt
estranged from traditional Judaism and married a Non-Jew. However, later
on, according to Jessie's autobiography, after having revisited her old home
town in Russia, she became a Zionist and planned to go to Palestine with her
friend Jessie. This plan was not realized; instead, she lived and worked at
Gould Farm, which is a cooperative rest-home still functioning in Great Bar-
rington and which is similar to Jessie's own Rest Home (Beth Jeshah) in Givat
Brenner (Palestine). It is interesting to note that Mary's own family seems to

Jessie E. Sampter, 1906

In the years of the budding twentieth century, when their own hopes and plans were budding too, the two girls used to meet once a month at the house of an elderly spinster who, herself, was an experienced writer and whose personality seems to have been greater than the few books which she published. She was Josephine Lazarus, the little known older sister of the famous American-Jewish poet, Emma Lazarus, whose inspired verses on the base of the Statue of Liberty in New York harbor welcome the newcomer to America and seem like the first symbol of the New World.

Josephine, Jessie's friend and mentor, had not only written the first biography of her famous sister, after Emma's early death; she also wrote two significant little books which reveal in what manner her influence may have been felt by young Jessie and her friend Mary, who, at that time were groping their way among the different religions and philosophies of the century. We owe to H. E. Jacob, the author of *The World of Emma Lazarus,* the discovery of this unusual woman and Jewess. While Emma's younger sister Annie, who later on became a devout Catholic, tried to obliterate every vestige of her sister Emma's important role as a poet of Jewish ideals, Josephine seems to have been a whole-hearted Jewess, for whom the development of the religion of the prophets meant the religion of humanity. In Jessie's later interpretation of Zionism as a "dream of a regenerate humanity" we seem to find something like an echo of these early talks with Miss Lazarus.

In those years, the two enthusiastic girls used to go all the way to the Lazarus home on Tenth Street, and as Jessie was still suffering from the aftermath of her polio attack, Jessie's

---

have been unacquainted with this inner attitude of hers. Her sister maintained that she remained estranged from Judaism like the rest of her family. Mary Antin ought to have been made the subject matter of a biography herself. In her last years Mary's quest for a faith went out to oriental idealism. She worshipped a Hindu prophet, Sri Baba.

sister, Elvie, who always took motherly care of her ailing sister, faithfully trudged along. She was highly rewarded by being allowed to listen to their stimulating discussions. In fact, Miss Lazarus sometimes asked for Elvie's reaction to a topic, telling her that she (Elvie) represented the "average listener," a comment which Elvie never forgot. Among Jessie's unpublished manuscripts, we have discovered a draft of an Introduction to an edition of Josephine Lazarus' *Essays.* They seem never to have been published, which perhaps we need not regret too much, as Jessie confessed in this draft that, in spite of all her love and admiration for Josephine, "the woman herself was greater than all her writings." These literary afternoons seem to have stimulated Jessie's own writing activity and to have clarified her thoughts. Eventually, Jessie found her own way of thanking her literary mentor; her first major publication *The Great Adventurer* is dedicated to "J. L." (Josephine Lazarus).

It seems to the present-day reader of this slender little book as if Jessie Sampter had come a long way from her amateurish verses in *St. Nicholas Magazine* and the conventional summer poems of Arverne to this significant, though decidedly youthful, book. In nineteen chapters of ecstatic prose-poetry, evidently strongly influenced by Walt Whitman, this booklet tried to portray a peculiar sort of "Great Adventurer" in this world of ours. Who is he? Neither Cortez nor Vasco da Gama, as you might think. The hero of this brave little booklet is every child who by his birth automatically becomes a member of the endless chain of beings in the gradual development of the cosmos. Here is all the joy and pride of the 19th century scientific "Genesis" of the world. The mechanistic universe replaces the ancient legends of former centuries. Tennyson might have written these enthusiastic verses. They represent the proud, overproud answer of the science of the 19th century to the enigmas of nature. In Jessie Sampter's life, they play a

more important role as they represent the Credo which remained her own and grew old with her:

> "I love this fearful world. I trust the Unknown, because it is
> the whole of myself. The space holds me; and the darkness
> spreads a great light. For this is the bottomless pit and the roof-
> less heaven and in it I am forever."

Taken as a whole, this little book is a marvelously youthful
work; it certainly reveals that illness and bodily handicaps
could not curb the indomitable spirit of the young poet.

It is gratifying to see that the little book was favorably received by the American press. "An affirmation of Self-Faith"
it is called by an anonymous reviewer, who winds up his enthusiastic words with these lines:

> "One is sure to carry away from the reading of this little book
> a keener sense of his spiritual power and a heightened desire to
> express it in some creative action. . . ."

It is true, there is not much originality in this mechanistic
genesis of the individual as a chain in the gradual development of the cosmos. Contemporary critics could not but notice
the influence of Walt Whitman and of the Bible on Jessie's
hymn-like prose style, but for the biographer of Jessie Sampter
it remains an important testimony to the victory of a human
soul over an ailing body. And in this sense, *The Great Adventurer* fittingly stands on the threshhold of Jessie Sampter's own
adventures in life and thought.

III

The Seekers

Unless one sees a glimpse of truth at fifteen, one is not likely to discover it later.
. . . But most grown people have forgotten, how they felt at fifteen and are apt to underrate the mental processes of boys and girls. I myself at that age felt so keenly the lack of sympathy in older people that I made a point of writing down certain experiences. . . . At fifteen, we all think ourselves exceptions, no matter how commonplace we may be now. . . . At fifteen, one craves something that can relate and shape all thought. . . .
The Seekers.

While Jessie Sampter's first book *The Great Adventurer* roams on the wings of her "insatiable soul" through the eternity of time and space, her second book takes the reader right back into the homelike atmosphere of the Sampter family house, where the "solemn dreamy child" grew up in the midst of a group of friendly, boisterous cousins and friends.

The Seekers, published in 1910, was quite unusual. "This is a live book!" the author begins her first chapter. "It was lived first and written only afterwards." Jessie herself was well aware that "this book did not lay any claim to art"; it was a philosophic adventure, an educational experiment "written down by one, but lived by seven."

To understand these somewhat mysterious words of introduction, it will have to be remembered that young Jessie — she was about twenty-six years old at that time, was not only a poet for whom each experience turned into a song, but a born educator as well. Throughout her whole life, she was eager to experiment not only with words as a poet, but also with souls, preferably young ones, as an educator. We must remember that in later years in Palestine nothing intrigued her more than the new experiment with human souls, the collective living which she saw in the Kibbutz. In the same way in which she advocated the Kibbutz as an experiment in collective living, she offered this little book as an experiment in "collective thinking." She considered those group discussions, which she valued throughout her life, the surest means of exploring the minds of her young partners in the game.

In the "Old House" which Grandpa Sampter had built in 1880, Jessie had been surrounded by cousins and friends, male and female. In this book we find a group of those same youngsters crowding round their young teacher and group leader, just as in former days the cousins had flocked around her when she told them one of her famous stories under the chestnut tree. Some of the six "Co-Authors" whom Jessie mentions in her preface, are still alive and have assured this writer that the legend of a "live book lived by seven and written by one" was by no means merely a literary device, as one might imagine; it was no more than the truth.

THE GROUP OF YOUNG SEEKERS

In the modest apartment where Jessie and her mother lived after her father's death, four young girls and two boys (all of them between fifteen and seventeen years old) used to meet every Sunday afternoon with Jessie, their admired teacher who was not much older than her students. The book which grew out of these meetings was a sort of spiritual drama, and the author introduces the different persons in her first chapter as if they were actors on the stage: dark and mysterious like a young "Arab"; a lover of beauty and art; a dreamer and a hero-worshipper; a vacillating soul who might become a society-belle in later life; the daughter of a Jewish father and a Christian mother, who is an enthusiastic follower of Christian Science; a young student who has much to say, but is not yet able to say it all. In the center there is Jessie, as discussion leader and teacher — but a "seeker" in her own way like all the others.

These seven well-educated and well-meaning youngsters had established the so-called "Seekers Club" in order to discuss questions important to all of them: questions of life and art, of religion and truth. They all had one thing in common. With the exception of Ruth, the Christian Scientist, they were all without any specific religious training, although — or rather because — they all came from cultured Jewish homes in New York. In other words, they all grew up in a home similar to the Sampter house, where the new creed of Ethical Culture had replaced the "old time religion." This feature, alone, would make this forgotten book valuable as a historic document depicting the atmosphere of American Judaism in the last decades of the 19th century.

It is quite significant that, at this time, the lack of religious training appears as a decided asset in Jessie's eyes. Her Introduction claims that "they were free from those clogging superstitions and false perspectives which result from an early training in any symbolic and fixed creed."

It was a somewhat bitter personal experience which made Jessie write this book, as her preface indicates. All the teenagers seemed to feel, so she writes, "that unless one sees a glimpse of truth at fifteen, one is not likely to discover it later." But most grown-ups have forgotten how they felt at fifteen and are apt to underrate the mental processes of boys and girls. "I myself," she confesses, "at that age felt so keenly the lack of sympathy of older people that I made a point of writing down and remembering certain experiences."

A most startling confession, if we remember Jessie's sheltered and carefully tended young life. Who were the "adults" who underestimated her "mental processes" while she was in her teens? It seems that her fine and sensitive mother could not regain her former interest in life after she lost her adored husband. Elvie, who was more balanced and less vulnerable than Jessie, may not have been conscious of it, but sensitive Jessie felt that she and her feelings seemed unimportant and immature to her mother and her mother's friends. So she had to write this book in order to get rid of the feeling of frustration and disappointment. It is a process that was to be repeated later in her life and that found its climax in her final belief in psychoanalysis as a means of overcoming depression.

Two problems, so it seemed to her and to her partners, needed a solution more than did any other problem in the confused life of her era: the lack of unity, of a common purpose, in the deeds of the community of men, and the problem of moral and religious education for children. It was to solve these problems that she had founded the Seekers Club. We have a clear picture of the Club proceedings: each member wrote a paper about one of those questions which specially interested him or her. These papers were collected by the discussion leader, and at the end of the sessions, Jessie surprised her listeners by telling them that she had composed a book out of these papers, in order to show the way to other seekers with similar problems. Incidentally, as one of the original "Seekers" told this writer, the original group violently resented such publicity, as they did not feel that their youthful outpourings were significant enough to appear in print.

THE INFLUENCE OF THE BOOK

At first, the modern reader of this little book might easily share the opinion of the original group. What did the seekers talk about in their heart-searching discussions? The reader cannot but feel somewhat disappointed. These youngsters did not propose to "set the world on fire." It is the Credo of the Victorian era which opens up before us: the world of George Eliot, of Dickens and Emerson, most of all, of Leigh Hunt and his eternal creed: the love of your fellow man. But one revolutionary principle seems to fill them all with the pride of the 19th century. They all felt assured that religion had to be replaced by research, faith by science. So they discarded the idea of personal immortality and substituted the idea of the immortality of the species. Taken all in all, *The Seekers* represents the credo of the young idealists of the Victorian era, which we have already discovered, more or less, in Jessie's first book, *The Great Adventurer*. Still, the discussions seemed significant enough to Professor Josiah Royce, the famous Harvard philosopher, who willingly agreed to write an Introduction to the little book.

This Introduction, in itself, is most revealing. At first, Royce confesses that he felt a little doubtful whether an experiment like this could accomplish anything; did not the discussion leader overestimate her partners? But in reading the book, he had to approve highly of the practical idealism that Jessie stood for; and he also admired the wise and skillful method of the discussion leader, which "proved itself." "The members of the Club will have their eyes opened by these hours of seeking values which are indeed permanent." "On the whole," Professor Royce continues, "the book is not only a vivid portrait of honest seeking at the beginning of our century, but of a wise author who contributed to the task of helping our nation to regain the much endangered and much confused consciousness of its own unity."

Indeed, Jessie might well have been satisfied with Royce's judgment; he seemed to single out the very reasons for her having written this book. This spiritual satisfaction seems to have been the only visible success of the book, for this educational experiment was not a literary or financial success. In fact, the author not only did not receive any royalties from her publisher; there were even difficulties in getting back the manuscript.

In spite of the financial failure, the young author may not have been displeased in later years, when looking back to this first experiment in collective thinking. It was the beginning of a long series of educational ventures, which formed an important part of Jessie's life and work. Without having tried this pedagogical experiment, she might not have made her first important contribution to Zionism, her School of Zionism. This same method of clarifying other people's ideas and views made Jessie invaluable as one of the first Zionist educators in America. And it all started when those six youngsters came to see her and she organized the Seekers Club.

Jessie's own fond hope that her book might be useful to other young people seems to have been a little excessive. However, it so happened that this writer was able to find some evidence that young people were reading and discussing the "Seekers" more than ten years after it was published. The copy which I read belonged to the Harvard Library, and on its fly leaf it bore some words of dedication from one reader to another reader. In 1920, a Mrs. Clinard gave the little book as a Christmas gift to her friend Miss Dee.* Now in 1920, Jessie Sampter had already "built more stately mansions" for her soul; she had gone to Palestine in 1919. But if she had happened to see the copy of her book in the Harvard Library, she would have been well pleased with the success of her "live book" which stayed alive at least ten years after it was written.

---

* Evidently, the two women had been discussing the same problems and so the older woman gave this book to her friend.

IV

Escape and Return

Whom shall I send? said the Lord.
"Not me, not me!
I am weary to death.
I am out of breath,
I see no reward.
Not me!"
Then whom shall I send? said the Lord.
"Another one!"
But my friend,
There is none.
If you are weary, sleep, sleep,
For the wind is rough, and the way is steep
And there's dust and ashes at the end.
But who will go and whom shall I send?
"SEND ME!"
The Messenger

While the young "Seekers" with their leader, Jessie, assembled in the living room of the Sampter apartment, Mother Virginia was lying ill in the adjoining bed-room, patiently and quietly as she used to do all things in life. She died in the late winter of 1909, and Jessie felt lonely, indeed, after she was gone. Elvie, her only sister, had married in May, 1906, given away by their 89-year-old Grandfather, Michael Sampter. Now Elvie and her husband, Edgar Wachenheim, lived in their own home; and though the two sisters remained devoted to each other and the Wachenheim's offered to share their home, Jessie's heart remained restless. For some time after her mother's death, she tried to stay near New York with their old German governess who had migrated to America and had become the friend of all the family. But after a while she returned to New York City and tried to find her way back to life and work.

Jessie had always had many men friends, but hardly ever a lover. Men usually singled her out because of her mind; some of them were taken with her marvelous eyes and her warm heart. In fact, in those lonely days after her mother's death, it seemed to her family and her friends that an unusually cultured young man, who had first been attracted by Jessie's poetry, was growing into a genuine friend, taking her out to concerts, meetings and the theatre as often as he could. Perhaps he would become more than a friend, Elvie thought in her motherly heart. And as Jessie seemed deeply in love with him, Elvie at long last took on herself the ungrateful task of openly discussing the matter with him. She found out that he, too, was attracted by Jessie's mind but not by her person. However, it speaks well for all the people involved that this man, in later life, after he had married one of Jessie's acquaintances whom she had introduced to him, remained one of Jessie's closest friends. It was this man who helped her, years afterwards, to adopt a little girl who became the joy and delight of her lonely days; and so, in some way, he tried to make up to her for the cruel disappointment his early friendship had unwittingly caused her.

Tentative Steps Towards Unitarianism

Perhaps it was this frustrated hope which made Jessie turn all the more eagerly to her literary friends. For a long time she had been attending the meetings of the well-known Poetry Society of America, of which poets like Edwin Markham, Edgar Lee Masters and all the better known poets of the day were members. They used to meet once a month at the National

Arts Club at 15 Gramercy Park. Jessie was much respected and
liked among the poets; to this day, the daughter of one of the
members has not forgotten Jessie's "pale, passionate, spirit."
Most of all, it was the President of the Poetry Society, Dr. Merle
St. Croix Wright, who was destined to exert a decisive influence on the life of the young "Seeker."

Dr. Wright was a connoisseur of great literary understanding. He wrote poetry himself and had translated the sonnets
of Heredia from the French. From the beginning, he had admired Jessie's poetry, in which he found an echo of the Biblical
Psalms, and he also admired her pluck in overcoming her
bodily frailty. But Dr. Wright, besides being a writer, also was
a Unitarian minister. For fifteen years he had been minister
of the Lenox Avenue Unitarian Church, and this daughter of
an agnostic, in her restless quest for a congregation with whom
she could worship, may have interested him as a God-seeker.

In those years, Jessie had explored various types of religious
service. After having lost the shadowy God of her early childhood and remaining unsatisfied by her father's creed of Ethical
Culture, she had gone to a Jewish Reform Temple, but she
found the services wordy and meaningless, at least for herself.
Then she tried to attend an Orthodox Synagogue; but here,
too, she did not fare better. "It was a strange service in a strange
language," she says in her autobiography. At last, she attended
services in the Unitarian Church, where she found her literary
friend, Dr. Wright, officiating. Here she discovered much to
attract her; it was the same disregard of ceremonies and dogma
and the same stressing of ethics which she had experienced in
her "ethical culture" home when she was a child. American
Unitarianism in Jessie's days did not rally around a creed, but
around a mental process by which each individual arrived at
his own answers according to his knowledge and conscience.
Some members of this group even regarded this system as a
return to the basic outlook of the earliest Jewish followers of

Jesus, so it is easy to understand why Jessie's homeless soul felt attracted to it and why she asked of her friend, Dr. Wright, to be admitted as a member of his congregation. In any case, when Dr. Wright, in 1911, wanted to introduce her to a young writer whom he greatly admired, he called her, "Miss Sampter, one of my parishioners."

THE DISCOVERY OF ZIONISM

Dr. Wright who was a keen observer of new literary talents, used to take new books as subject matter for his sermons whenever he thought them worthwhile and interesting for his listeners. So, one Sunday morning, Jessie heard him read from the pulpit a fragment of a new Jewish book which had just been published. He called the writer, "A Modern Prophet." Jessie remembered that some friend had brought her this new book, and that she had not yet got around to reading it. Now she went home and read it from cover to cover. She felt transformed. This was what she had been waiting for.

The book was written by a young Jewish poet, Hyman Segal, and was called *The Book of Pain Struggle.** Dr. Wright, much impressed with it, had planned to dedicate a whole series of sermons to it, and soon after this memorable Sunday he introduced Jessie to its author.

We are fortunately in a position to reconstruct this meeting. It occurred at a session of the Poetry Society. Dr. Wright introduced the two young people to each other, then spoke to others. Hyman Segal was, as he wrote me later, "flabbergasted," when Jessie, "the shy, slight, hauntingly smiling, utterly charming wraith of a girl" turned to him and told him, "As much as

---

* Its exact title: *The Book of Pain Struggle Called the Prophecy of the Fulfillment,* published by H. Segal in the 1840th year of the Diaspora and the 27th day of the 5th month of the 134th year of the United States of America (Massada Publishing House, New York).

Dr. Wright admires your poetry, I don't feel that he got your message, but I DID!"

In order to understand this somewhat enigmatic sentence we ourselves shall have to read Segal's book. *The Book of Pain Struggle* is the story of a modern "Pilgrim's Progress." Its hero runs away from home to find his "call." Neither the delights of love nor the loveliness of nature satisfy him; in the big city he meets with an initial success, but eventual failure. He takes to the road and at long last, in the desert, "where the strugglers of old, the pain-men of my people, saw their visions," he discovers an ancient parchment, a covenant. Now he calls and the voice answers:

> "In pain and struggle I sought thee,
> That thou bring faith to mankind.
> Go therefore in haste: For the land
> Languishes without its own people
> And man without his ancient faith."

When Jessie, the daughter of the agnostic, read these words, she felt, so she wrote, "as if a door had been opened to her."

But what is the meaning of her startling and provocative observation that Dr. Wright had not got the message of this book, while she had? After rereading the book, we seem to grasp her meaning: the Unitarian minister, cultured and humane, to whom the brotherhood of man was no mere phantasm, comprehended the first part of the message only, the message for Everyman, "to return to his ancient faith." But Jessie, the daughter of an ancient people, who had lost her way and had not been able to find it by means of her ethical culture, had to learn anew the ancient prophecy spoken to her own ancestors: that the land languishes for its own people. Well may she have felt that, as she termed it in Biblical words, "the live red coal had been pressed to her lips."

This meeting between Jessie Sampter and Hyman Segal was the beginning of a lifelong friendship. The Jewish writer was, as he recalls, somewhat taken aback, on seeing the American Jewish assimilationist surroundings in which his new friend lived. Segal came to see Jessie in her sister's house in New Rochelle and found her in the neighborhood of a Christmas tree and looking up to the Sistine Madonna. Jessie tried to defend the cultural aspect of both of these in their discussion. She had enjoyed the merry celebration of Christmas in her childhood, had even woven a sort of legend around it in one of her earliest poems, in *St. Nicholas Magazine*, while Raphael's Madonna represented, in her eyes, the highest and purest ideal of motherliness.

But now she learned to treasure the ancient symbols and customs of her own people. And it was Hyman Segal who introduced her to his revered friend, Henrietta Szold, who had a great formative influence on Jessie's life.

Henrietta Szold was, as Jessie confessed in later years, one of her three great teachers of Judaism in her pilgrimage through the world of ideas. In Miss Szold's house, she first perceived the beauty and dignity of Jewish religious customs. Sitting at her side in the synagogue, she came to feel the poetry of the age-old Jewish service. Dr. Mordecai M. Kaplan was the second of her "Masters." In the Saturday afternoon meetings in his house, which Jessie very diligently attended during the next few years, Dr. Kaplan opened her eyes to the historic significance of the Bible as a record of the gradual development of the Jewish spirit. And her greatest teacher, as she wrote, was the Jewish People itself, as she discovered it in the East Side of New York, in the Jewish Settlement House, where she later took her abode, "because she wanted to be among her own."

This was the great discovery of her lonely life; for the first time she perceived that she had a people of her own, a natural congregation with whom to laugh and to weep and to pray. She said in *The Speaking Heart,*

> "I realized the Jewish people,".... "I have a people, a congregation. It is not in the church nor in the synagogue. It is in the streets, in the tenements, in the crowded 'Pale' of Russia and Poland, in the little agricultural settlements in Palestine. . . . It is my people, a chosen people. God has called it, has chosen it for suffering and service. The God that is in me, is also in my people. . . ."

At first, Jessie objected to the mere idea of Zionism; she could not see how the Jewish problem might be solved "by a plot of land." But soon she understood that her own and Miss Szold's Zionism meant much more than mere nationalism. It meant salvation for the sick soul of the modern Jew. She understood that through the suffering and the resurrection of the Jewish People in their own land a new life and a new salvation (*geulah*) might dawn for all mankind. Her dream of Zionism was the dream of a regenerate humanity.

Jessie learned Hebrew in these years, and while she studied she could not help feeling that she was now learning something which she had known long ago and had long since forgotten. No wonder that her young teacher, the former Rivkah Aronson, who is today Mrs. Barnett R. Brickner, remembers clearly how Jessie went around like a hungry child imbibing every item of Jewish lore which she could lay her hands on: "What awakened in me, asleep for generations? I smell grapes, touch cool orange leaves, rest under a palm tree. . . ."

From now on, all her life belonged to one idea and one only; service to her Jewish People. "Zionism became her religion," her way to God.

V

War and the Pacifist

> Brother, my brother, I slew thee with
>   my hand,
> And spilt, to serve a righteous cause,
>   thy blood upon the land;
> Brother, my brother, I cannot understand
> Why I, to keep the Lord's command,
>   must break the Lord's command.
> *Brother, My Brother*

When the dire days of war came to the world, in 1914, they found Jessie Sampter in her new home in the Young Women's Hebrew Association on West 110th Street. All her American friends saw the War as a catastrophe far across the seas, looked at it like detached spectators who suffered with the unhappy afflicted, but then went their own way, happy and grateful that they lived in a country at peace. Jessie and Miss Szold felt differently. It was their own Jewish People, their own nation which was suffering in the Russian "Pale," in Germany and in Palestine. They feared the future of the Jewish settlers in Palestine might be endangered. Moreover, they recognized the threat to the very future of Zionism, whose moral, financial and personnel resources had come in the main from Russia and whose ideas stemmed largely from Germany. Now the mantle of the prophet had fallen on American shoulders, and the American Jews were not at all prepared for it. Zionism had been rejected and almost despised by the "upper middle class" Jews in America, just as it had been rejected by the same class of Jews in all the Western countries.

It was at this fateful moment that Jessie felt called upon to make a decision. Just as once before in her life, when she fell ill, she had decided to get up and ignore her illness, so now she resolved to meet this crucial situation by *action*. She made up her mind to educate the American Jew to Zionism.

In those dark days both Henrietta Szold and Jessie Sampter did their level best to perform this difficult task. Miss Szold "took to the road" and, as she herself expressed it, "preached" the need for Zionism all over the country. At the same time, Jessie created her "school of Zionism" and was much admired for this creation by her older and much more famous friend, Henrietta Szold.

THE GREAT INFLUENCE OF HENRIETTA SZOLD

It is one of the remarkable phenomena in Jessie Sampter's life, perhaps it is significant for every dedicated life, that she met, at every crossroad of her devious pilgrimage, exactly those people who were able to help and influence her. So she had met Josephine Lazarus who first roused her interest in her Jewish faith; so she had met Hyman Segal and his book. And now she encountered Henrietta Szold, the unique woman who was able to show the way to a searching soul like hers. We have seen how Miss Szold, by accepting her into her own household, helped Jessie to see the beauty and dignity of Jewish tradition and so became one of her teachers of Judaism. Now we shall see how Miss Szold, in the dark days of the war, helped the younger woman to find her way out of the despair which seized her when she realized that Jews everywhere were in mortal danger.

We do not know the exact date of the first meeting between the two women who were destined to walk side by side through their strenuous lives. This much we do know; it must have taken place soon after 1912. In that year, Miss Szold and her mother made their memorable trip to Palestine and saw the disease-ridden children there. That trip led to the founding of Hadassah, the Women's Zionist Organization dedicated to the "healing of the daughter of my people."

It was a rare friendship that grew up between the two widely different women. Henrietta Szold, thirteen years older than Jessie, came from the traditional home of Rabbi Benjamin Szold, beloved by Jews and Christians alike; Jessie had grown up in the house of a brilliant father who was an agnostic and in whose home Christmas and Easter had replaced the Jewish holidays. But in spite of these differences, the two women soon discovered that they had a world in common; in fact, these very disparities gave to their friendship a special flavor. For these were the years when, as one of her friends told me, Jessie was intent on assimilating every new and hitherto unknown item about Jewish life. Not only did she "quiz" her friends most unmercifully; she, who two years ago "had not even known when Yom Kippur would come," tried to live the life of an Orthodox Jew. Her family and her friends were somewhat bewildered by this startlingly new way of life; but her devoted sister made it possible for her to keep the Passover holiday in the way Jessie wanted to keep it, by getting new dishes and keeping them separate. It seemed to Jessie, in those years, that the Jewish People urgently needed this "fence around the law" in order to keep apart from the nations of the world in the centuries of the Jewish exile. Later on, in her years in Palestine, Jessie somewhat modified this point of view.

It is a genuine loss for the friends of Jessie Sampter that her letters to Henrietta Szold are not available at this time; perhaps they will turn up at some time in the future, when Miss Szold's Palestine papers have been classified. But until that future day, we shall have to be satisfied with Miss Szold's letters to Jessie, which Marvin Lowenthal published in his invaluable book, *Henrietta Szold — Life and Letters*. In fact, by interpreting these few letters, we shall gain insight into the gradual development of the friendship of the two correspondents and the influence of Henrietta Szold on the life and thought of Jessie Sampter.

Two vital ideas were conveyed to her younger friend by the daughter of the Baltimore rabbi. We have already suggested the first: the importance and beauty of Jewish tradition. The second, and perhaps even more influential for Jessie's further development, was the message of Zionism — religious Zionism as the first generation of the *halutzim* understood it, not mere nationalism, but the dream of a religious rebirth of mankind, a "regenerate humanity" as Jessie termed it.

When did Jessie's conversion to Zionism occur? Did she owe it to Hyman Segal's book or to Miss Szold? Was this the "message" which Jessie had in mind when she told Segal about Dr. Wright and herself? Again, we do not know the answer. However, we shall find some hints in Lowenthal's book and others in Rose Zeitlin's biography of Henrietta Szold. Last, but decidedly not least, we shall learn much from Jessie's *The Speaking Heart*, the first chapter of whose second part is entitled "War."

It is clear that, once Jessie had grasped the cogency of an idea, she would have to go all out for it. But it would seem from the earliest letters that Miss Szold did not quite know for certain how best to make use of Jessie's outstanding gifts for the benefit of the great Jewish popular movement which united these two women. Miss Szold's first letter to Jessie, dated July 15, 1913, and published in Lowenthal's book, mentions with satisfaction Jessie's meeting Alice Seligsberg and the "Folder Propaganda" which owed its birth to the two of them. The idea was to propagandize the basic tenets of Zionism by means of small booklets to be distributed at nominal cost at every Hadassah meeting.* But this was not enough for Miss Szold. She goes on to speak of her own joy and satisfaction at the idea that "Jessie is going to write":

> I am glad that you are going to write. You will serve Zionism best in that way. I believe it is what we need most — good writers from whose work Zionism will radiate as a fine aroma. We have had the brochures, the Apologia, the party pamphlet, the disquisition, the essay — now we should have literature based on Zionism as a pervading conviction and life-philosophy. . . .

All this was planned before the War broke out. The catastrophe of 1914 threatened havoc to Zionism, as Jessie and Miss Szold understood at once, though America still hoped to be allowed to remain at peace. Zionism was built on international community work, and Miss Szold confided to her friend that she was "not a little anxious about our own practical work." It is likely that fears such as these moved Jessie to renounce her poetic plans and to take up practical work. During the dark years of the war, her own education in Zionism and the creation of the School of Zionism, in which she herself taught, fully employed Jessie's frail bodily powers. Friends of her poetry might regret that so much of her effort was given to her educational work in the "School" and the creation of her well-known Zionist manuals, the first of which also originated in the war years. On the other hand, the history of American Zionism ought never to omit the important role which Jessie Sampter, the educator, played in those dangerous years.

Miss Szold, the only person able to criticize her, was, of course, full of praise for Jessie's educational efforts. But at the

---

* "Nationalism and Universal Brotherhood" was the title of one of the "Folders" written by Jessie Sampter. It was the reprint of a talk which she had given at the Open Meeting of Hadassah (New York, Shavuot, 1914). It explained that the meaning of Universal Brotherhood included the brotherhood of nations and answered the charge of narrow nationalism directed against Zionism. Jessie's article is accompanied by a note which explains the name of Hadassah and records the Basle program.

same time, her motherly heart could not help fearing that Jessie "would try to do too much" (March 27, 1919). In her memorable letter of September 6, 1919, she had, in the early years of their friendship, stated the basis of their relationship and its value for herself:

> *Koah* (strength) — that should include everything, but one cannot help being specific and personal. So I wish for you . . . and it is a wish for all of us . . . that strength of body may be added to strength of mind and spirit, so that you may be able to grasp every opportunity and miss none to make your gifts available for the Jewish cause. I, for my part, am grateful that you and I were brought together. May the years cement the friendship and knit us firmly to each other for whatever the same developing years may show to be the good and the true.
>
> I owe you much; I want to owe you more. But if strength should not come in the measure in which I wish it for you, then at least husband what is vouchsafed to you, for we need you. . . .

This is indeed a significant letter. It contains all the elements which knit the two women together: all the motherly care of the older for the younger woman, all the awareness that Jessie, the poet, could perform great things for the Jewish cause, which Miss Szold herself could not perform, and that Jessie's gifts had to be made available for "whatever is good and true." This letter is like a program of their lifelong friendship, which grew and grew till the day when Henrietta Szold had to bury her younger friend and to tell the children of the Kibbutz in Palestine what a friend they all had lost.

VI

As Student and Teacher of Zionism

Are we willing to be good soldiers, to follow? To lead, if at all, not because we
choose, but because we are chosen? Are we
willing not to stand upon platforms and
shout to a crowd, but to sit together in a
little room and study maps and figures? It
is intensive work without glory. For both
teachers and pupils it means digging
trenches, digging in the dark, digging for
light. . . .
— Report to the Hadassah Subconvention on the School for Zionism, June
1915.

Jessie, before starting to educate other people in
Zionism, first had to educate herself. Again it was Miss Szold
who sent her friend to a man who was better able than she to
open Jessie's eyes to the historic development of the Jewish
spirit during the centuries of the past.

He was Dr. Mordecai M. Kaplan, and we already know that
Jessie Sampter counted him as one of her great teachers of
Judaism. Of the three teachers whom she often gratefully
mentions in her letters, Miss Szold had been the first and near-
est to her heart; but Dr. Kaplan, to whom Miss Szold had sent
her, proved even more important for Jessie's concept of
Judaism and Jewish history. Dr. Kaplan vividly remembers
Jessie's eager attendance at the Saturday Afternoon Discus-

sion Group which met at his house during the war years in 1915-16. They discussed, among other things, "the meaning of religion." Luckily, some of the minutes of these meetings, conscientiously taken down by Jessie, have been preserved in Dr. Kaplan's archives and have been made available. Unfortunately, owing to her uncertain health, Jessie had to miss some of these meetings; but whenever she was able to attend, she certainly made her presence felt by her alert and provocative participation in the discussion.

It may have seemed to her that here she found another circle of "Seekers." She could not but perceive that these new Seekers were widely different from the bewildered and confused youngsters who had made up her own former "Seekers Club." These young men and women had a clearly defined attitude towards Judaism, and they had come to Dr. Kaplan to learn from his wisdom a new approach to the age-old doctrines of the Jewish past. In these years, Dr. Kaplan first formulated his new term for the ancient religion. Kaplan's notion of a Jewish civilization stressed the social and humane implications of our faith rather than its dogmatic aspects. Jessie, who, from her earliest days had taken a keen interest in human relations, welcomed this new approach, and the other members of the group, who are well-known in American Jewish circles, also did their share to enliven the discussion. There was Horace Kallen, whose sister Deborah, now in Jerusalem, became one of Jessie's closest friends; there was Alice Seligsberg, her partner in learning Hebrew; there was Lotta Levenson, Miss Szold's friend and co-worker in Hadassah efforts, who now lives in Jerusalem.

Jessie herself explains what she hoped to get out of these discussions. She wanted a clarification of the foundations of religious belief, and she also wanted to know the place of Jewish nationalism in American life. Did she want to get more arguments to defend her own position against the attacks of the "fear psychologists," as she termed them? Again, she disarmingly and frankly reveals her own main interests: not in ideas, but in human beings. So she does not hesitate to confess that religion, in itself, interests her less than the religionists. Again she is looking for her congregation, the community of believers, as she was in the days of her meeting with Hyman Segal.

It would seem as though she wanted to pursue her quest and gather more answers for the questions of her friends who opposed Zionism. Often she mentions her childhood-religion, Felix Adler's Ethical Culture, with a sort of respect; she calls it "the American religion par excellence" and is afraid that, like Jesus and St. Paul, this new religious leader might turn against his mother-religion. Religion itself, so she repeats again and again, is to her a social experience; and in the minutes of the last meeting of the series (March, 1916), she cites three prominent American Jews as typical of present day American Judaism: Kallen, the apostle of "cultural pluralism"; Brandeis, the dedicated Zionist; and Mary Antin, whom, as we have seen, she had to defend against the attacks of the other members who only saw the *Promised Land* and Miss Antin's marriage to a non-Jew but ignored her later development. Out of all these discussions and teachings Jessie gradually developed her School of Zionism.

THE SCHOOL OF ZIONISM

In July, 1914, in speaking to the "Graduates of Young Judaea," Jessie announced the new School of Zionism that Hadassah was planning for the coming year.* This undertaking grew to sizeable dimensions in the following years, and brought forth not only the "School" itself, but the famous Zionist manuals: the *Course in Zionism* (1916), the *Guide to Zionism* (1920) and *Modern Palestine, A Symposium* (1933).

---

* *The Maccabaean,* July, 1914.

These Zionist text books form an important part of Jessie Sampter's literary-educational work. The well-thumbed pages of surviving library copies testify to the fact that they were really "live books," as Jessie had called one of her earlier efforts. An entire generation of young Americans read them and was influenced by them.

There is some irony in the fact that these Zionist manuals were, in the market-sense of the word, Jessie's most successful books. They were the first to need new editions. One has only to look at the different size of these books to understand how much conscientious work the editor put into their preparation: the *Course* (published 1916) has 95 pages. Its second edition, the *Guide to Zionism* was published in 1920, after the author herself had just left for Palestine; it had grown to 262 pages. Its third edition, the *Modern Palestine* took the form of a "symposium," and that, in itself, was a proof of the success of its message. One has only to glance at the distinguished names of the co-authors in order to understand why the form of the manual had been changed. For, with the passage of time, Zionism had stood its test. It had proved, not to the joy of the Zionists themselves, that the Jews of the world needed a haven like Palestine, needed it bitterly. The third edition of the Zionist Manual revealed the reaction of the world to this life-saving idea; it also had to show what had been accomplished in Palestine. So Albert Einstein, Norman Bentwich, Nahum Sokolow, Henrietta Szold and many others, came forward to testify to the need for Zionism and to its achievements. "It is the right time to take stock of the Zionist enterprise," said the review in *The Nation* after the publication of this third edition.

All these manuals grew out of the modest "School" which Jessie had announced in July, 1914.

Alice Seligsberg, writing of the beginnings of the Zionist efforts in a Hadassah *Newsletter,* revealed how, through Jessie's educational enterprise, the hitherto rather amateurish Zionist activities were infused with new life. Sewing classes, choral groups, seeds sold for Palestine; all these were laudable, but could not be compared with Jessie's educational program. Her "School" offered three courses: club leadership, public speaking, Zionism. It was, as we see from this program, a school for future leaders who had to learn the basic elements of their leadership themselves. Their background was different: they were teachers, students, working girls, business women or housewives. They met one evening a week. Jessie, as the director of the school, presented a report to the Hadassah Subconvention in June, 1915, when the School had been in existence for about six months. In this report she soberly and modestly, though not without a certain pride, defined the character and the aims of her entire educational work:

"We are not educating dilettante Zionists. We are training our army, our reserves. . . . I am willing to use the terms of war, however I hate the frightful fact, because I believe the nobility, self-sacrifice and loyalty aroused by war can be aroused by other calls to national devotion. . . .

"We have good generals. Many are willing, and a few are able to lead. Can we follow our good generals with devotion and obedience to the cause they serve? Are we willing to be good soldiers, to follow? To lead, if at all, not because we choose, but because we are chosen? Are we willing not to stand upon platforms and shout to a crowd, but to sit together in a little room and study maps and figures? It is intensive work without glory. For both teachers and pupils it means digging trenches, digging in the dark, digging for light. . . ."

Perhaps it would not be meaningless once more to define the special "brand" of Zionism which is contained in these text books. Of course, we easily understand that in these text books Jessie put to use what she had learned in Miss Szold's home and in her discussions at Dr. Kaplan's. It is not narrow-

minded racial *apartheid*. On the contrary, this Zionism of the
first generation opened its eyes wide to the neighbor who "is
like you," according to Jessie Sampter's translation of the
Biblical commandment *Veahavta le reakha kamokha,* (Love
your neighbor; he is like you). The attitude of the Jews towards
the Arab neighbor in Palestine was shaped by these ethical
views; the Arab was the neighbor and had to be treated as such.
Of course, that generation did not live to see the War of Independence in Palestine, nor did it live to see the State of Israel
with its predominantly Jewish population. They certainly may
have imagined it different in some ways; but they would have
been overjoyed at the *kibbutz galuyot,* the ingathering of the
persecuted Jews, which proved Israel's basic right to exist.
Jessie Sampter's words about her Zionist aims are as meaning-
ful today as they were when first she uttered them — meaning-
ful for the handling of the Arab minority, the Arab refugees,
and most of all, for the acceptance of the persecuted Jews from
the Orient, which the new state has gathered into its borders.
True, history may have bypassed the early theories of a bi-
national state. But it has by no means made invalid Jessie's
dream of Zionism, as she often expressed it in her letters:

"The dream of Zionism as we dreamed it in America was
the dream of a regenerate humanity. The Jewish nation in
Palestine was to be not only another nation, but a distinctive
nation, to bring salvation amid the orgy of injustice and violence. It was to be our experiment in righteousness. . . . More
than that — we would find God again in the land where He
first set His name; find Him not only in ceremonies and prayers
but in a *way of life that would praise him with its fullness.*"

THE BOOK OF THE NATIONS

The School of Zionism and the Zionist manuals were two
of the three great tasks which Jessie Sampter set herself in
order to survive those years of the war. There loomed another

task for her in the background of her mind: "a book had to be written" . . . or rather transcribed from the ancient prophets into the language of our days, by a modern daughter of the ancient prophetic people.

The genesis of this book was different from that of the other books of Jessie Sampter, because she felt that it was not she who was writing this book, but that it had come to her, from beyond. In reading this chapter in her autobiography it would seem that now, for the first time, she understood the meaning of the Biblical reference to the "burning coal" which was handed to the prophet Isaiah by the Angel and pressed to his mouth.

In 1917, during the horror of the weeks when it became more and more apparent that America could not keep out of the War, Jessie, as she tells us in her autobiography, lay on her bed one morning "so faint and weak that she had no courage to move."

"Suddenly, a great awe filled me, and a whole series of connected thoughts sprang full grown from my heart.

"There was a book ready to be written, created in an instant, from the surging, teeming depth of heart and mind.

"I had not conceived it. It had come to me from the depth under the depth, from the Under and Over about us, of which we are only aspects and instruments.

"I wanted to write it in Hebrew, but though the idea was Hebraic, I had not the words.

"For a month I took notes, feverishly as if from memory.

"Then came Passover: I lived in a nebulous world of creation. Passover week, except the Holy Days, I wrote, wrote. . . . For three weeks after I wrote steadily every morning. In the afternoon, I moved among persons, I spoke, I was living in a world apart, exalted, not feeling, but being, writing as one who is possessed. . . ."

Miss Szold sacrificed a whole evening to a reading of this

"Book" and urged publication; so did Jessie's sister. By the time Jessie returned from the Zionist Convention in June, the book had already been accepted by a respectable firm. Again, it must have seemed to the author that somebody else, not she herself, wanted the book published. It was put out by E. P. Dutton and the reader at Dutton's, an Englishman, understood what was in her mind and "that she had not written it, but only transcribed it from the language of the ancient prophets"; so he put on the title page "Transcribed by J. S."

"An interesting, unusual man. A Christian, a religionist. I could speak to him on matters of faith more easily than to most Jews (or any, I might say, except Miss Lazarus and Mary. . . . Yet ours is the spring of faith. . . ."

In these words from Jessie's autobiography, we seem to sense both the mental anguish in the heart of the peace-lover and the intense feeling of inspiration which moved her to write this "obsessed" book. For the slender little volume which she had written as if somebody had dictated it to her represented the answer of the pacifist to the cruel problem of war, given in modern words, but in prophetic rhythm.

Evidently, the reader at Dutton's whom she mentions was a man who understood her, as few of her friends did; he may have been the author of the interesting "Publisher's Note" which preceded the volume:

"The *Book of the Nations* is in effect a message — a spiritual message so vital and urgent that in its delivery the methods and even the words of those fiery message-bearers of old, the Hebrew prophets, seem the most natural vehicle of its expression, the writer being, as it were, but the *mouthpiece of a greater Power. . . ."

No better appreciation of the book could have been given. However, the publisher was a man of the world; and so he by no means expected that the American public would easily accept this message.

"The publishers realize that some will dislike the *Book of the Nations,* and some will resent it, and that others will frankly despise it as Jewish; but they themselves feel that in the *Book of Nations,* a voice that has been all too long silent makes itself heard with compelling beauty and that this outwardly unassuming little volume is one of the most remarkable products of this strange and significant crisis in the history of man. . . ."

The strange little book contained nothing more or less than a new chapter from the Bible. It is somewhat gratifying to note that the Publisher whom we quoted above, also took a dim view of the volume's prospective fate at the hands of the critics. A review printed in the Mizrachi magazine called it "noteworthy both for its thought and for the manner in which the thought is expressed. Indeed, it is so exquisitely conceived, so vibrant with feeling and written with such felicity of expression that one can hardly bring oneself to speak of the work in prosaic terms. . . ." The same reviewer praises most of all its " 'liberality of thought.' Is God a personal God, is He the God of Jew or Christian or Buddhist? Through Israel are the nations of the world to be blessed — it is Israel who is to give to a dying world the word of life."

Let us hope that Jessie read this review; she would have been gratified in the period of depression which followed the elation of writing the book.

The first chapter of the book contains a new version of the story of the flood. God is planning to destroy the nations, just as He destroyed them in the times of the flood, because He abhors their greed and hate against each other. But there is one nation which objects to His plan and reminds Him of His promise: Israel was to be a blessing to all the other nations. In the end, He agrees to spare the world because of His promise to Israel. God, after all the despair of the present, repeats His promise in spite of His disappointment with the nations; yes, even Israel too, is a "grovelling, degenerate Jewry."

This little book reveals the despair in Jessie's heart during

the war years, and it reveals something even more significant
— her utter loneliness in the world of her American Jewish
friends. It seems as if she must have been immersed deep in a
well of loneliness, being the only (or rather one of a very few)
lovers of Zion in the midst of her own fellow-Jews "who wanted
to be slaves in the good country where God brought them to
live in." This is a bitter and painful summing up of the attitude of American Jewry at this time. The book was indeed the
utterance of a prophet in the wilderness. No wonder that her
American friends were startled by it. It revealed how far, how
very far from their own world, this much beloved and admired
girl who lived in their midst had drifted.

> You say: God has freed us at last from whips and scourges.
> Our masters give us rest. Now will we be good slaves. Now will
> we be a 'Light among the nations,' a soft, diffused light, not burn-
> ing with too fierce a flame. Why should we go into a land that
> is waste? Our lot is good, where God has set us down. We shine
> with the brightness of much gold. . . . We will not move. . . .
>   "You say: I have bought freedom. Leave me alone."
> Yet the freedom you have bought is slavery. The gold you paid
> is your SOUL.
> You patronize the Jew driven to you from other lands.
> You think by much charity you shame him and glorify yourselves.
> Hence you say:
> The Jews are not a nation: they are a charitable society.

Here certainly is the echo of many a discussion between
Jessie and her friends and relatives. Only from this book can
we understand that the young prophet of Zionism became a
slightly embarrassing person to her friends; they may have felt
a little guilty, but could not respond to Jessie's fiery message.
This was a sad farewell to the friends of her youth, the people
of the Ethical Culture.

However, her outspoken book did not leave the reader
entirely without hope for mankind: God renews His promise
at long last; and the scourge of war shall vanish:

Now, on this day, I will give you a new weapon . . . the sword
of the spirit.
And all the nations shall praise God in their own way
And Israel shall worship the Lord our God in the way of Israel
forever and ever.
Arise, oh Watchman, said the Lord, arise and proclaim it:
For the day dawneth. . . .

Of course, part of the publisher's prophecy came true: this
unusual book, though favorably received by the press, sold
poorly and remained absolutely unheeded by the politicians.
It would seem that this failure to reach her goal brought about
a bitter depression in the soul of the author. Her mental balance seemed upset, and for a while she fell prey to the fateful
experience which she later called "The Vision." For a while,
she seemed on the verge of insanity.

IN A MORE HOPEFUL VEIN

Once more, she and her friends tried to reach the ear of the
public. They combed through her numerous poems which had
been published in various magazines during the prior decade,
and in 1919, a small selection of Jessie's poetry was published
under the significant title: *The Coming of Peace.*

These poems seem to the present-day reader even more significant than her passionate outburst in the *Book of the
Nations*. In deceptive simplicity they speak the language which
Jessie knew best: the language of the heart. Some of them we
shall find in her *Brand Plucked from the Fire*, her collection
of poems written in the course of thirty years and published
in 1937. Others had to be omitted in 1937, since they dealt
with topical events and hopes that had been proved illusory
by the course of time. Thus, the very impressive poem "The
Hundred Million," bore witness to the short period when
Jessie and Miss Szold — and several more millions of "dudes,"
as Jessie later termed them in a semi-skeptical word — were
deluded by President Wilson's famous address in 1918. They

had not become happier by their deviation from pacifism, as Miss Szold wrote in her letters. Jessie soon reverted to her life-long conviction: a detestation of war, which she meant to stand as a watchword over her whole life:

"Brother, my brother, I slew thee with my hand
And spilt to serve a righteous cause thy blood upon
   the land.
Brother, my brother, I cannot understand
Why I to keep the Lord's command
Must break the Lord's command. . . ."

It is a gratifying thought that these melancholy songs did not remain the farewell note with which Jessie parted from her native land before she left for Palestine in 1919. For before that day she once more returned to her best friends, to the children who loved "Aunt Jessie" and whom she loved. One more book appeared in these years, and this is what she wrote on the first page of this collection of songs, prayers and children's poems, which she called "Around the Year in Rhymes for the Jewish Child."

"I dedicate this book to Jewish Children, especially to
two of them, Edgar and Jessie" (who were her sister's
children).

These simple rhymes, neither the most original nor startling poems written by Jessie's pen are among the books which remained alive after the author's death, as we shall see in a later chapter. They accompany, in simple, melodious verses, the whole Jewish year with all its feast and fast days. They certainly show that the author had come a long way since those early days (1900) when she had written her prize-winning poem about the Christmas Tree for the *St. Nicholas Magazine*. Jewish teachers soon discovered that there was no better way to interest their children than by these simple songs, and Jessie would have been well satisfied to hear that some of her Jewish children songs are alive and being reprinted today long after her death.

VII

The Vision

> Lord, I am weak and small; my weak
>   hands are unfit to do Thee service
> Lord, I am hungry and unsheltered; my
>   will is greater than my might.
> But Thou has not deserted me,
> Thy word is very nigh to me,
> Thy spear has been within my heart
>   so long;
> I wait — I serve Thee with my words,
>   meanwhile;
> I wait — I serve Thee with a singing heart;
> Lord, I am ready. SPEAK.
>   *The Call*

Before Jessie Sampter could realize her dream of going to Palestine, she was destined to undergo a strange mental experience which might easily have wrecked her plans and her life, too. In *The Speaking Heart* she called it "The Vision." It seems to have been one of those peculiar parapsychical experiences which occur in the lives of many poets; they are inexplicable in terms of logic, but are as infinitely valuable for their poetic world as they might be dangerous to the poets' mental equilibrium.

It was 1918. Jessie had carried a full load of work during all the war years. She had organized her School of Zionism, had taught her classes, had written the first of her Zionist manuals. Henrietta Szold, her motherly friend, had often warned her not to overtax her strength; it was none other than Miss Szold who had suggested that Jessie take one whole year off and stay with her sister in New Rochelle, so that she might have a complete rest and become better fit to do her work in the future. This, however, proved to be financially impossible; the war prices had cut Jessie's income in half, and she felt compelled to earn at least half of her living. So she accepted a paid position which the Zionist Organization had offered her. It was the same work which she had done without pay and most willingly before; now it helped to pave her way to Palestine. Later, in 1919, she was sent to Palestine as a literary reporter for the Zionist Organization of America, as it would not have been possible for her to get a passport without having a definite task to fulfill in Palestine.

But before then the strenuous work of the last years and the deep mental anguish caused by the War made themselves felt. First an attack of pneumonia compelled her to leave her work and to let her willing sister nurse her. Then her sister, too, became ill and had to go to the hospital. But a trained nurse, a devout old Lutheran, took care of the ailing Jessie. Gratefully she reports in her autobiography how both of these women helped her to lead the traditional life which she wanted to live.

However, in 1918, all the strain and anguish which she had suffered and which had been distilled in her prophetic book, the *Book of the Nations,* caused a strange nervous illness, a breakdown, which almost led this sensitive soul to the verge of insanity. With admirable lucidity, this illness is described in Jessie's autobiography — proof of the sober American common sense which went hand in hand with the vivid imagination in the soul of this poet.

It is interesting to note that, in the first decades of our century, the time of the First World War, experiences like this "Vision" of Jessie Sampter's occurred frequently and in different countries. It seems that, in the War years, the wish to reach the borders of the unknown grew with the longing to get in touch with dear departed ones. Thomas Mann, in his *Magic Mountain*, mentions such "ambiguous efforts," and the Austrian poet, R. M. Rilke, whose poems have recently been translated into English, believed in "automatic writing" and the revelations given to him by the "Unknown Lady" (*Die Unbekannte*), whom he had never seen, but whose voice "spoke to him from the ouija board."

It so happened that, in the early years of the War, two of Jessie's friends, who had travelled extensively in Europe, became interested in this same sort of experiment. They acquired one of the currently widely publicized ouija boards, three-cornered wooden boards, which were supposed to possess occult power to contact the souls of the departed and to answer questions addressed to them by giving signs of "Yes" or "No," by moving or by indicating the letters of the alphabet. The ouija board which Jessie mentions in her autobiography seems to have been without lettering, but answering to questions by a movement of the board to the right or to the left. Jessie was keenly interested to know if her departed mother, whom she adored, would approve of her recent return to Jewish tradition and of her plan to go to Palestine. In her autobiography, Jessie told her readers that these experiments were successful, but that she felt they overstrained her nervous system. She resolved never to repeat them.

Evidently, her resolve was too late. Some days thereafter she awoke in the morning feeling that "superhuman power" had been given to her. Questions asked by her without words, only by concentrating on them in her mind, were answered by a throb in her temples. In this way, she experienced what she later on called her "Vision." It may have been a parapsychical impression similar to the psychical experience of poets like Rilke. She herself called it her "Cosmogony"; and it seemed to her that she heard an echo of her own favorite ideas about Life and Death coming out of the Cosmos. A strange hierarchy

of angels was revealed to her, and they joined her in prayer-
song, when she started to sing the *"Adon Olam,* the beautiful
prayer-song of the Sefardic poet."

> The dead do not die. When we die, we return to a state of
> infinite and joyous being, out of which we came; but we return
> other than we came, because of the life we have lived. This life
> is creation. In it, God is making us. . . . What we gain in this life,
> and retain at the end, we shall never lose again . . . God is God:
> He cannot be explained or described. . . .

These are some of the thoughts which were revealed to her
in her "Vision." They repeat her own life's creed; just as
Rilke's revelations reiterated his own basic beliefs about life
and poetry.

Meanwhile, her devoted sister was deeply depressed and saw
in Jessie's "trance" an attack of a serious nervous disease. In
vain she tried to get in touch with her; Jessie felt that she had
to concentrate on the questions in her mind that she was unable to answer. At last, her sister brought a medical friend to
see Jessie, and he suggested that they consult a nerve specialist,
a psychiatrist.

This man helped save Jessie's mental equilibrium. They
asked him whether, under existing circumstances, he would
agree to her undertaking the dangerous and difficult journey
to Palestine. Contrary to their expectations, he strongly advised them to let her go, as her whole heart was set on this
fulfillment of her lifelong dream. He shrewdly suggested that
she pledge herself to go for one year, not more. Only after this
initial test, should she decide whether to remain or come back
to America. If anything should go wrong, he promised "to fix
her up." (This, incidentally, proved more than he was able
to perform. He was in Europe, when Jessie tried to see him
after one year in Palestine.)

PLANS FOR THE FIRST TRIP TO PALESTINE

From then on everything seemed to move smoothly towards the fulfillment of her goal. "Her little big sister" and her brother-in-law hated to see her go; but now, understandingly, they did what they could to facilitate Jessie's way. Her sister shopped with her as if she planned to buy her "trousseau." It is a little sad to see how Jessie, herself, took up the idea that she was "married to Palestine." In choosing her outfit, she indulged her preference for lighter and more colorful dresses, as she saw herself already in an Oriental environment where she would not feel out of place with her colorful garments. All her friends gathered around her and gave her a magnificent farewell party. Some of them, like Henrietta Szold and Mary Antin, were hoping to go, too. Still, not all the clouds had vanished from her mind. Long ago, in her childhood days, as she now confessed in her autobiography, she had sometimes harbored the haunting fear that she might lose her mind, the typical fear of a vivid imagination. Even in this case, she persisted in holding on to her Palestine dream; there is an Insane Asylum in Jerusalem too, she thought; and better there than here.

Jessie never again went through an attack of these psychic experiences. Miss Szold came to Palestine in 1920, soon after Jessie's arrival, and reported to Jessie's sister in her own inimitable sober and reliable way. Jessie, so she wrote, seemed neither better nor worse than when last seen in New York. None of her psychic experiences had returned, so it would seem that an understanding physician and an equally understanding family virtually saved Jessie's mental balance by letting her have her way and realize the dream of her life by going to the Holy Land.

This "Vision" obviously represented a danger never quite

absent from Jessie Sampter's own life and her thoughts. But
at the same time it supplied her with a key to all the mental
anxieties and worries of youth in Palestine and anywhere else.
She never would have been able to minister to the many ailing
young souls if she had not herself experienced the dangerous
affinity of vision and mental crisis. Zionism and the magnificent achievement of her dream to share in the upbuilding of
a homeland in Palestine — these were the powers that saved
her and brought her to the fullest self-expression of her personality.

I quote a letter which she wrote to her sister on leaving, and
a little poem which she also addressed to her sister, both of
which significantly express her feelings in the last days before
leaving America.

> New Rochelle, New York
> July 16, 1919.
>
> Dearest Sister:
>
> Before I leave for Palestine, I wish to supplement with this
> letter some of the provisions of my will — and to say a few other
> things. I write in the full consciousness that my not returning to
> America is among the likelihoods, either because I may not out-
> live the year of probation, or because at the end of that year I
> shall have found in Palestine that spiritual fulfillment, that
> "at-homeness," and that opportunity for full-hearted service
> which I expect to find there and which would necessitate my
> staying. This consciousness makes my last days here with you
> very hard, but also very wonderful. I have never had the home-
> feeling anywhere since I was twelve years old*; perhaps I never
> shall. I seem always to be standing on tiptoe at the edge of an-
> other, a different world. Perhaps Palestine, like the world of my
> childhood, will be nearer that world.
>
> You know that to me death is merely one of the changes or
> adventures of life. I cannot and do not wish to think of it
> otherwise. I am nearer to that which is all — and always present
> is the consciousness of certain very definite physical dangers of
> which I have purposely not spoken to you. I do not know whether
> you know of them. If any accident befalls me, remember that I

---

* Since her father died (1895).

preferred that danger to my safety here. But safety is nowhere and would be the negation of life.

I am leaving my old journals with you, and I must leave it to you whether or not to destroy them. I do not care. I have been transformed since I wrote them. I am not ashamed of my many confessions of weakness. Also I have no desire to preserve them unless they prove to have more than a personal value.

Of the letters in my boxes, some may be worth preserving — for example, Mary Antin's — but do not keep any merely out of deference to my feelings.

I wish nothing in this letter to bind you in any way. It merely expresses my desires at this date. One thing you will know without my telling you: if I should die in Palestine, I wish to remain buried there.

You and I are very much alike, in many things. I know you will understand even the strange things in this letter. You may speak in different terms than I, but you know how wonderful life is as well as I do; and you know it is not counted by the term of years.

I am with you always, here or anywhere!

Your loving sister
JESSIE E. SAMPTER

VIII

Discovering Palestine

O little land of mounting crags,
Of lonely height and deep,
A world away thy children stray
And long and wait and weep.
O little land of holy men,
Of fearless dream and deed,
From clime to clime
The storms of time
Have strewn thy hardy seed.
I know the golden oranges
Englobed beneath the moon,
The sky that spills 'twixt seas and hills
Its shining draught of noon,
The vines that bind the valley's brow
With grapes like jewels set,
The silver green of olive sheen —
O, can my soul forget!
                    The Promised Land

"The Providence I believed in gave me a travelling companion; friendly, delightful, comforting. This was Ethel's* father, going to visit her, a white-haired, straight, proud old gentleman. He called himself my 'Protemporaneous Daddy' and his humor, gentleness and his practical vision about persons and the appealing quality of his age gave con-

---

* Though *The Speaking Heart* is autobiographical, Jessie changed the names of her friends so that, for instance, Alice Seligsberg appears as "Ethel," Henrietta Szold is called "Giborah," and Mary Antin is called "Sarah."

tent to six weeks of travail as well as travel that would have been a nightmare otherwise. . . ."

Thus Jessie Sampter ushers in the next chapter of *The Speaking Heart,* a chapter that treats the beginning of a new life for her, her life in Palestine. We know the man whom she describes in such glowing colors; he was old Mr. Seligsberg, father of Alice Seligsberg, the friend of Miss Szold and of Jessie. Alice had not only learned Hebrew along with Jessie; she had also preceded her in journeying to Jerusalem. At that time she was living in Jerusalem as a Hadassah worker.

Providence added to this impressive traveling companion, another one, no less engaging and a member of the Sampter family to boot. He was her cousin, Emil Simon, who to this day (1953) remembers the pleasant conversations he had with his much-admired cousin, Jessie, on the deck of the "Adriatic" when he had brought her a comfortable deck chair. Together they enjoyed the breezy air and the ever-changing configurations of sky and clouds. Some of Jessie's letters portray her buoyant, excited mood:

S. S. Adriatic
Sunday, August 17

Dear Edgar,
Dear Sister:

This is the first time I am not too lazy to write. My laziness is only part of my general feeling of comfort and well-being; I have not rested so thoroughly in years. To say I am comfortable is to put it mildly. I consider that I am living in luxury; and as, besides the various stewards and stewardesses, I have four men ready and anxious to serve me, I scarcely move hand or foot except to get in or out of bed. I am now on deck, where Emil procured a chair for me on the best side of the best deck, which chair the steward moved to the exact spot where I wanted it, beside my traveling companions. Mr. Seligsberg is sitting besides me. He is a dear old gentleman, and has provided me with light literature and Maillard's candy. . . . My cabin is very comfortable and pleasantly situated, just in front of the dining salon; air as good as at 190* with the addition of a salt tang. . . . No

* 190 Webster Avenue, in New Rochelle.

machinery anywhere in the neighborhood. I took your advice and stayed in bed most of one day, had my breakfast in bed, but went to the other meals, as I am so near the dining-room. I am eating aplenty; the table is ample and good, and one can get anything one asks for including very good eggs. . . . I had a bare hint of seasickness; since then I have been perfectly well. . . .

The children's daily letters are a joy. I am sure I cannot convey to them my appreciation. . . .

Emil has been very attentive and helpful. . . . He has introduced me to . . . some Boston people who have been in Palestine; the mother — who is a Christian Scientist — drew me out in a way that I am sure amused us both and probably did us some good. Emil has insisted on showing them my book; got it out of my trunk himself. By the way, he helped me unpack. Otherwise, I have so far succeeded in not meeting any one. My traveling companions improve on acquaintance. I want to get to know them well. We have a table to ourselves. . . . If the trip continues as well as it has begun, you need have no worry.

The latter part of the journey, however, seems to have taxed Jessie's strength to the limit. The world was still dislocated by the aftermath of the war: crowded trains, in which travelers had to sit up all night, a starving Europe. By the time she finally reached Palestine, Jessie, in spite of all her enthusiasm, was "glad to be alive," and soon had to recuperate in the Hadassah hospital. There, on the second day after her arrival, she met the woman who was destined to share her life in Palestine and become her best helper, Leah Berlin.

Jessie, in later years, described this unusual woman in an essay called "Watchwomen" (*Jewish Frontier*, Nov. 1936). Leah Berlin was an exile from Russia and had been so well trained in communal work that, during the war, when all Jews in Palestine who were subjects of Allied Countries were banished by the Turks, the British officers turned to this woman, whom they had seen organizing the people and taking care of them, and asked her to continue her activity. Now she was organizing a factory in Jerusalem in order to give work to the idle and starving girls there. Jessie, in her article, gives us a picture of how Leah looked in the war: simple and straight, her black braids folded like wings over her ears.

Leah Berlin wrote to me about her first meeting with Jessie. At first, they seemed worlds apart, for Leah only spoke Russian and Hebrew and very little English, while Jessie spoke English and very little Hebrew. But soon they found the way to each other, never to part again. When Leah's mother came from Russia to Jerusalem they took a larger house and Jessie moved in with them. Before that time, Jessie had lived in the house of a young couple from New Rochelle, Dr. and Mrs. Segal; they, too, became Jessie's close friends, and she adored their little son, who may have reminded her of her own little nephew, Edgar, to whom she had dedicated her book of *Rhymes for Jewish Children*.

Nevertheless, the first winter in Jerusalem was more than difficult for the frail woman. We would not know about its hardships did we not have her unpublished autobiography. To get the whole truth, we have to compare her letters to her sister, which in Jessie's own words, "contain the truth, but not the whole truth," with this manuscript.

Here are some fragments from her letters:

Jaffa, Palestine, September 23, 1919

Sister dear, and dear Edgar and the Kiddies,

Here I am, safe and sound, as you will have known long before this letter reaches you, by the cable which I have sent to the Zionist Organization, including the request that you be notified.

And I am happy, too, very happy. We arrived early yesterday morning; I arose at dawn and saw the sun rise over Jaffa as we approached, and at about 8 o'clock we came ashore. I am not going to describe for I shall have to do that in print, and this particular description will appear in the *Young Judaean*, in "Miriam's Journal." However pleasant it may be to do, I consider it work, and I am not going to work for you. Nellie Straus ... came out to the boat to meet me. We went to the shore in a row boat rowed by a dozen or so sturdy Arabs. After passing the

---

* *Young Judaean*, December 1919 — December 1920.

formality of the customs, we found a carriage awaiting us —
ordered by Nellie — and while our trunks were carried off,
strapped on a camel's back, we drove off through the heavy sand
and dust of picturesque but dirty old Jaffa — the Arab bazaars
and markets are a delight to the eye and a horror to the nose —
to the Jewish suburb of Tel Aviv. Here I have a large, airy and
comfortable room in a very fine but terrifically expensive boarding house — PL5 a day — but it's only for two days, as tomorrow
we expect to go up to Jerusalem. There I am to stay for a week
or so at the Medical Unit house, until I can make other satisfactory arrangements.

So far, being here means to me all that I dreamed it would.

There are a number of tots here at the house, with whom —
will you believe it? — I hold Hebrew converse. Just now, they
are collecting stamps in blank books, and it is funny to hear a
tot of five and a half, who cannot yet read, tell correctly where
each stamp comes from. We are quite near the Mediterranean;
it is a sandy shore, with a few palms and forced gardens, and
airy, square white stone, red-roofed or flat-topped houses. I am
busy today. My play days are already over. So I must stop. . . .

Much love to you all from

JESSIE.

On October 1, she wrote to her sister:

. . . . As for the land itself, I could not have imagined it. It is
wonderful beyond words. I had heard that its beauty was in
soft coloring and light and atmosphere, but to hear and to see
are two different things. With all the discomforts . . . and there
are many . . . I find life here in Jerusalem marvellously restful
and peaceful. I love to be here more than I have ever loved being
in any place. I shall not describe now, because gradually I shall
be writing everything for print, and I hate to repeat . . . but the
glamor of the Orient, the camels, the beautiful Arabs in their
bright clothes, the gay Eastern bazaars in the Old City are a
sensuous joy to me. And I feel thoroughly at home, especially
in this warm, soft climate with its vitalizing sun and its mountain breezes.

Tell Mrs. Segal for me to bring all the things I told her . . .
mosquito netting, rubber bath-tub, insect destroyer, toilet paper.
. . . Tell her also to bring powdered milk for Boysie, as there is
still a milk shortage.

As I look back on the trip, it seems almost a nightmare, and
this is the fulfillment of a dream. I am very happy and very unhappy . . . the latter because of conditions here.

> But even if I were not a Zionist and if I did not love the land,
> I should want to be only here, because it is so intensely interest-
> ing and there is so much to do.
> Life is too big for letters. . . . Much, much love!

In Jessie's letter of October 1, we see for the first time the
two sides of life in Palestine, which at the same time harassed
and attracted her: "It is intensely interesting" and "there is so
much to do." These facets were to be the pivots of her life
during the next few years.

Another source tells us about Jessie's "dangerous but serene"
life in these first years in Jerusalem. Miss Szold, in a letter
which I owe to the courtesy of Jessie's sister, summarizes Jessie's
physical and mental state in these first trying years in Jerusalem. Writing soon after her own arrival in Jerusalem (May 30,
1920), she says:

> Jessie is one of the serene ones. Indeed, she is more wonderful
> than ever. Her thoughts are purged of even the last alloy, if there
> ever was any. There can be no doubt of it, she is perfectly happy
> here. She seems to feel that she has found exactly her setting.
> Her pen cannot keep pace with her brain. She is full of ideas,
> practical projects and fancies. . . .
> She has a wonderful friend — wonderful as a woman and won-
> derful as a friend — Miss Leah Berlin. She is a large woman, large
> physically and spiritually, built on large lines in every way, and
> her admiration of Jessie is whole-souled. She has poise — good for
> Jessie. She can bring Jessie down to earth, when it is well for her
> not to soar. As you know, they share a room, and that room is in
> the house of a New Rochell-ite. Altogether, you can dismiss all
> worry on Jessie's account from your mind. She is surrounded by
> friends, new and old.

She closes her letter with these comforting words:

> . . . . Don't worry about Jessie. If anything should go wrong with
> her, you may be sure there are many hands here to help her.
> But she is so happy, that nothing could go very wrong.

"She is so happy. . . ." Miss Szold must have felt, as many of
her friends felt, that Jessie Sampter was "where she wanted to
be" and was happy. But there was an obverse to this picture.

Now and then, we find a tell-tale sentence in Jessie's letters to her sister, which usually stress all the joy and peace which she feels in the Holy City. She tells her, for instance, that she "is very happy and very unhappy in Jerusalem, because of the conditions here." What exactly were these conditions?

HOLY DAYS IN THE HOLY CITY

When Jessie came to Jerusalem in 1919, she arrived on the eve of the New Year (*Erev Rosh Hashanah*). Soon after, she described her first bitter-sweet impressions of those days in an article which was published in the *Menorah Journal*. She welcomed the Holy Day at first all by herself from the window of her room, "looking westwards and southwards over the rolling hills toward Bethlehem and Hebron, over the white walls, and roads, the rose of sunset on the mottled hills, and the tall grey cypress trees and silver olive trees. And I knew the land was holy because its beauty cannot be told or said. It can no more be imagined than the melody of a song still unheard. . ." She dressed in white and set out to find companions to celebrate the holiday with her. But she was to be bitterly disappointed.

Neither candles on the table nor blessing of the wine reminded her of the days in the Jewish boarding house where she had lived. Looking for a congregation with whom to merge her prayers, she did not find a place in which to worship in all of the ancient and new Holy City. True, there were quite a number of synagogues. The Hasidim, the Yemenites and the other Oriental Jews prayed in broken-down old buildings, and their women had to content themselves with staying behind in an adjoining room, where dirty dishes were stacked on the table. She felt it below her dignity to pray in such surroundings. So, before Yom Kippur, she had to discover that "the special brand of religious Zionism" which flourished in America was not to be found in Jerusalem. "The Modern Zionists do not pray at all; and the *Adukim,* the Orthodox Jews, do not allow their women to pray with them. . . ." "I love these Jews: I revere their faith, their *emunah* (faith); I hate their precepts, their *dat* (law)." That was Jessie's first impression of the Holy Days in the Holy City.

However, immediately after Yom Kippur, a new spirit animated Jerusalem. A hush seemed to be lifted. Succot, the gay festival of the booths, was in the air. One saw men carrying *lulavim* (palm branches) and boys coming in from the country laden with pine boughs. . . . The Succah arose, a square booth with a roof of green boughs. In a Sefardic household she saw one Succah which delighted her. It was made of striped Oriental hangings of many colors on the outside, and of white sheets on the inside, through which the colors shone in the sunlight.

Succot week was a holiday week there. And the highlight of Succot was the gathering of the Maccabeans, the young Jewish boys and girls from all parts of the country. This was the "festival of festivals," for Jessie; for it represented the ideal of the new Jewish youth, a "healthy soul in a healthy body." Only now did she feel comforted for the loneliness which she had felt in the synagogues. And as if to confirm her belief in Israel's future, one of the non-Jewish lovers of Zion was in Jerusalem during the month of Tishri to talk to the Jewish women and make plans for the Hebrew University.

He was Professor Patrick Geddes, a "Scotchman, Botanist, Sociologist, Educator, Town planner, Visionary." It was his own suggestion (or his inspiration, as Jessie calls it) to address a group of English-speaking women on the problems of the University and their share in solving them. These meetings took place at the home of Mrs. Eder, a doctor and psychoanalyst, who was Jessie's close friend and physician. It was Patrick Geddes who made Jessie see a new Judaism in this ancient holy city, where so far she had found no place to wor-

ship; "a religious revival with social justice and equality."
Perhaps, so she felt, it would be the women's task to bring
about this religious revival. And only then — as in olden times
— "Jerusalem shall still give forth the Law and Zion instruc-
tion, and shall rejoice in the Torah of our Lord."

With the name of Edith Eder, we have introduced one of
the few human beings who illuminated those first years in
Jerusalem. Taken all in all, Jessie must have suffered excruci-
atingly, both mentally and physically. Only now can we understand why she called this chapter in her autobiography "Dust
and Ashes." She loved the land; never again would she leave
it, as she wrote to her sister. But what she did not write, or only
hinted at, was that she was deeply disappointed by its inhabitants. Later, in a calmer mood, she spoke of the "Errors in
Utopia."

The first of these "errors" has already been explained; it
was the negative approach to religious Judaism which she encountered in the Holy Days in the Holy City. She found either
extreme Orthodoxy or absolute rejection, and she sadly missed
her own brand of "religious nationalism." It was Geddes and
his hope of a religious revival who helped Jessie take heart and
wait "for the coming of Messiah."

But the second flaw in her Utopia depressed her even more
bitterly. This was the failure of the Western Jews to accord
social justice to their Yemenite brothers.

The Yemenites

The Yemenite Jews lived like pariahs in their native land;
humiliated and persecuted, and yet not free to leave. Many
of them had wandered for weeks in and out of the desert, des-
perately trying to reach a port from which to embark for
Palestine. The real start of their return to the Holy Land took
place about forty years before the famous "Operation Magic

Carpet," which, in our days, took them on "Eagles' Wings" to
the State of Israel. In 1910, a young Palestinian pioneer called
Yavnieli brought them the message of Zion, and some six hundred Yemenites made their way to Palestine. From then on,
there was a steady trickle of Yemenite immigration.

Now the Yemenites had some substantial advantages over
other Oriental and European immigrants. They spoke Hebrew
as well as Arabic; they were at home in the landscape and the
climate; and they were used to all sorts of hardship. On the
other hand, their social views as to the position of women and
children were decidedly medieval. In Yemen, women were
beasts of burden as well as child-bearers. In the polygamous
Yemenite household, women performed such labor as grinding
corn, repairing the clay huts and carrying water from the well,
while their lords and masters sat at home and "learned" the
Talmud. In the Palestine of 1920, as Jessie Sampter saw to her
disgust, these frail hard-working women were being exploited
by the earlier colonists. While the Yemenite boys learned
Talmud in *heder,* in the traditional, more or less old-fashioned
way, the little girls were made to take on domestic positions as
soon as they were "graduated" from kindergarten. Here, as in
their native Yemen, women and children "slaved," while the
boys and their fathers "learned." Sometimes, whole families
lived on what these domestic slaves earned.

Jessie saw all these happenings with a deep sense of horror.
Still, what she saw was valuable for her, for it revealed to her
where her own field of activity lay, and how much she was
needed. Frail and town-bred as she was, she could not build
the land with her two hands, as was the ambition of every
halutz or *halutzah* (pioneer). Instead, she tried to ameliorate
the lot of these so-called "stepchildren of the Jewish people."
Soon she established evening classes for the Yemenite working
girls, whom she, herself, taught. Later, she added discussion

groups for adults. She was more than proud when she succeeded in directing discussions in Hebrew, as she had ever so
often done in English. In fact, this may have been one of the
reasons why, after some years, she left Jerusalem, in spite of
all its attractions, for, in the village of Rehoboth, where she
later settled, there lived a large colony of Yemenites.

IX

Activities in Jerusalem

> Life here is full of excitement now. It is
> a wonderful fulfillment after the dark days
> we have been through, and the dramatic
> events one reads of in history seem most of
> them, pale beside it.
>
> Jerusalem, July 7, 1925

Another important field of activity, in addition
to her work with the Yemenites opened up before the eyes of
Jessie Sampter in the first years in Jerusalem — Scout work. It
had always been near to her heart. In her first report from the
Holy City after the holidays, she had found in the meeting of
the Jewish youth group, the Maccabeans, her best comfort
after the dire disappointment of the earlier weeks. Now she
found in Jerusalem, itself, one of her old friends and co-work-
ers in this field, Dr. Alexander Dushkin, who was kind enough
to send me some of their correspondence from those years. He
had taught in her School of Zionism during the years of the
War; now he happened to be her neighbor in Jerusalem and
soon they joined in Boy Scout work. In those years, Dushkin
wanted to organize Hebrew Scouts in Palestine. Jessie, as he
gratefully remembers, was very helpful to him. Together they
altered the Baden-Powell versions of the Boy Scout Manuals
and tried to give, instead, a more Hebraic face to the whole
movement. They added Biblical slogans and symbols and tried
to Hebraize the whole movement. The new scouts called themselves the "Tzofei Zion," while the earlier scouts retained their

old name of "Tzofim." Jessie wrote an elaborate Code and
Manual for the Tzofei Zion which, unfortunately, both Dr.
Dushkin and I have been unable to trace. An impressive letter
of Jessie Sampter's to Rabbi Eugene Kohn (November 2, 1920)
clearly reveals her aims in re-organizing the Tzofim: "to introduce Jewish in the place of purely military forms of social
organization as described in the outdoor life of the Bible. . . ."

In 1920, Dushkin took a whole troop of the Tzofei Zion to
Rehoboth, and there, much to Jessie's satisfaction, the first
Boy Scout Work-Camp of Jewish children in Palestine was
organized. The boys earned their camp expenses by working
half days in the vineyards and picking almonds. This was
Jessie's idea, as Dushkin gratefully remembers, and it was
Jessie who valiantly tried to keep the Tzofei Zion Movement
going when Dushkin had to return to America. Though she
failed in these efforts, some of her ideas were later revived in
the Chicago Jewish Sunday Schools, as Dushkin wrote to me.
This fellow-worker of Jessie's continued to prove a real friend
to whom she turned when, in the '20's, she was seeking addi-
tional funds for her Yemenite work. It is indeed a moving
thing to watch how, in her letters to Dushkin, she stubbornly
continued the struggle for the Yemenite kindergarten and
evening classes, which could not have survived without financial help from America. Some poignant passages from these
letters should be quoted. They illustrate the situation and
Jessie's indefatigable efforts better than any comment could
do. Such was the financial situation in the '20's that Jessie had
to look to a miracle for its solution.

> Rehoboth, August 22, 1928.
> . . . . I feel as if I were sending you an SOS call. It looks now as
> if we should have to discontinue the evening school for the
> Yemenite girls this autumn because I cannot raise the necessary
> funds for it, and there is none to help me. All I would need to
> carry on for the whole year is a little over $200. I have enough
> for the kindergarten lunches, which come first — and I do believe

you may be able to get it for me, from private sources, if not from the Keren Ami. I need it by October!

Your teachers made me smile, rather bitterly, when they said Hadassah and the Department of Education ought to provide for the needs of the Yemenites. The fact is, they don't and can't; and if I, as an individual, cannot raise the money, these children will go without their most primary needs. It is not a question of theories, but of human beings.

I get all I do get from friends who are not Zionists or whose gift does not conflict with their Zionist donations. As I have already taxed these to the limit, it is hard for me to raise what I need; it is impossible.

I turned again to the Vaad Hatarbuth of the Workingmen's Association, and asked them to take full responsibility for the evening school, as they are paying half the teacher's salary now. They refused; they have not the funds.

Please find a way to raise this money, or part of it, for our evening school. There must be so many persons in Chicago who would be interested and able to help.

October 19, 1928

Dear Mr. Asher:

When Dr. Dushkin cabled me "Friend sending forty pounds" I wrote him on that same day a letter full of the joy and relief I felt. I did not know who this friend was, but I knew he was a "friend indeed." For we were facing the possibility of having to close our evening school altogether for lack of funds. I had funds then for only two months; but the teacher had consented to begin on that in the hope of the miracle happening. You were the miracle.

SNOWBOUND IN JERUSALEM

One more item added to the difficulties of Jessie's first winter in Palestine: a blizzard and snowstorm, which she vividly portrayed in an article, "Snowbound in Jerusalem." Everyone had to help in bringing the bare necessities of life to the starving inhabitants of the collapsing houses. Teachers had to dig through the snow to bring at least bread to the Yemenites, who were snowed in without anything to eat. They came upon one oldster sitting in a corner with a big book studying in spite of the icy cold. "We bring you some bread!" they told him. "Do I need bread when I have the Torah?" he stoically replied.

Jessie, however, was not unaware that there was another side to this heroic picture. There were the Yemenites who, when one of them was slightly injured from having fallen off a roof, laid down their shovels, exclaiming "You see? God does not want us to get rid of the snow! He put it on the roof, so let it stay there!" Worse still: there were Jerusalem Jews, unwilling or unable to dig, who said out loud, "Let Arabs or the Yemenites do the work." However, these were the exceptions; many others — teachers and engineers — heroically did their best to protect the people from the falling houses.

So even the snowstorm had its lesson for Jessie. It seemed to her the duty of the American Jews, blessed with a better education and with abundant means, to help rebuild the fallen houses and to feed the starving Jews of Jerusalem. "If we will it, the harvest that follows this year of storm and snow will indeed help to feed the people of Jerusalem."

Jessie Sampter did not know that, in those days of snow and disaster, a special gift had been given to her. A little girl was born in Jerusalem whose parents were unknown. Not three days old, she was found in a basket before the door of the Jerusalem Orphanage. The nurses called her "Tamar Sheleg" (Snow), because she had been discovered in the days of the snow. This was Tamar, the little girl whom Jessie, some years later, took into her home and her heart in place of the daughter whom fate had denied her. With the financial help of an American friend she adopted Tamar Sheleg and the girl became Tamar Sampter. All of Jessie's later letters are full of joy and gratitude, for the "miracle" which had been granted her with this little daughter. This was the hidden blessing which the snowstorm had in store for Jessie's lonely heart.

Jessie and her adopted daughter, Tamar

POLITICAL BACKGROUND

We do not hear very much about politics in Jessie's letters to her sister. She naturally did not want to frighten the sister who had so much feared her going to Palestine. Whenever there were Arab riots, Jessie sent off a cable to her family, so that they knew about her own safety. In the spring of 1920 there occurred the notorious "Passover riots," which could not but reveal to the newcomer that her own vision of Ishmael and Isaac living peacefully together, each under his own vine and fig tree, was far from being fulfilled. There is hardly a word about them in her letters to her sister. But Leah Berlin, who at that time was living in Jerusalem with Jessie, told me that "the whole city was in great danger and that each night they expected to see the Arabs invade the Holy City from their headquarters in Hebron." An eloquent echo of these riots in Jerusalem is preserved in Jessie's article, "Arabs and Jews in Palestine." Though this article was written some years later, in 1923, it shows that she was fully alive to the gradual deterioration of relations between Arabs and Jews and deplored it. She had always liked the Arabs (sometimes even more than the Jews, because as a friend suggested half whimsically, she did not know them as well as the Jews). She loved their colorful Arabic garments, their festivals, their Nebi Musa pilgrimages, which, as a Hebrew scholar told her, must have been somewhat like the ancient Jewish pilgrimages to the temple in Jerusalem. The background of the riots seemed to her a political one, with Arab delegations traveling all through the land and also through America to plead their cause against the Jews. In the country itself, Arab peasants and Jews seemed to her to understand each other and to work quietly side by side.

Why, with those manifest signs of hatred . . . do Arabs and Jews still work together on the land, buy and sell and trade in

all the necessities of life and act in all private relations precisely as they always have acted?
Here comes my Arab egg woman, riot or no riot, barefooted, arrayed in a flowing indigo robe . . . over the white kerchief her pearly teeth smiling a greeting.
Hate there is; but it flourishes elsewhere. . . . The Jewish settlement from the beginning was of advantage to the Arab peasant, which they were quick to perceive . . . (Arabs and Jews in Palestine . . . quoted from her manuscript) .

Jessie Sampter — like all of us — had to unlearn a good deal of this happy belief in the following years; but she never wavered in her conviction that it would be possible for Jews and Arabs to live peacefully together. It may be interesting to note that not only a peace-loving woman and a poetess like Jessie, but a politician like Weizmann and a scholar like Dr. Judah L. Magnes shared this confidence.

Jessie's letters from the summer of 1920 breathe relief and hope. After the pro-Arab English High Commissioner Sir Ronald Storrs left, England had, in all fairness, appointed a Jewish High Commissioner, Sir Herbert Samuel, who was enthusiastically welcomed by the Palestine Jews, as the "Messiah ben Joseph," the precursor of the Messiah ben David, who would usher in the Messianic age. Jessie Sampter described his entrance into the Holy City in a colorful article for the *Young Judaean,* called "Twentieth Century Legends."

July 7, 1920.
Life here is full of happy excitement now. Even though I go out not at all, the echoes of it come to me here. Sir Herbert Samuel seems to be all that we hoped of him. The feeling is complete that our fulfillment has come, that a new era has begun and that now all depends on our capacity for work and the intelligent support of Jews all over the world. It is a wonderful fulfillment after the dark days we have been through, and the dramatic events one reads of in history seem most of them pale beside it. It is a drama that has lasted two thousand years — no, more — and the news of San Remo's decision came in the midst of a fast day proclaimed in mourning for the riots and in protest

against our imprisoned self-defense. The fast was literally changed into rejoicing. Now comes a Jewish governor, who so far has satisfied all by his fairness, a Zionist and a leader.

Jerusalem, July 12, 1920

The political situation continues satisfactory and full of promise. Every one is satisfied with the Jewish Governor, the intellectuals have surprisingly little to criticize, and the superstitious have already woven a web of legend about him that is marvelous. They call him the forerunner of the Messiah. . . . What I am hoping and waiting for, is constructive work, peaceful, busy life, an immigration of the tired, heartsick Jews from Eastern Europe, a chance to plant fields, build houses, educate children. It should come soon. I am sick of all politics. I think they are a kind of fever, a symptom of sickness. What matters is how people live and work together. . . .

July 21, 1920

The other day we were discussing Jerusalem with some Americans, and we remarked that, if Jerusalem were in America, it would be known as a summer resort. There is no doubt of it. I had heard of the breezes here and the cool nights, but I never conceived of anything so beautiful as the spring and summer weather here. So far, I have slept only one night without a blanket. Of course, the noonday sun is hot — I do not go out in it at all — and we have had perhaps a dozen days of *Hamsin.* "Hamsin" means fifty, because there are supposed to be fifty hot days in the year. These days are very warm, even in the shade — say from ten to four o'clock — but they are nothing like our muggy days, and the breeze is almost constant. Just now — ten a.m. — it is delightful. The most wonderful blue sky, with flecks of tiny clouds, and a soft breeze. It is moonlight again; the nights are intoxicating. While the Nile is flooding from winter rains in South Africa, we often have heavy clouds chasing over the sky and strong winds, but never a drop of rain. Nor is it ever damp, except at night from the dew.

So much for the weather. I am still not over the frequent attacks of intestinal trouble, which the physicians all seem to agree are nervous. Still I am much better. I get quite a bit of work done in a leisurely way, and I am taking a sort of semi-rest cure, going out hardly at all. I have just decided to leave Jerusalem again, in about two weeks, and spend the month of August on Mt. Carmel overlooking the Mediterranean. There is a good Jewish hotel there, there are woods, a marvelous view and always cool breezes. That way it is even cooler than here, com-

bining sea and mountain. My woman physician has just gone
there for a few days and she will make all arrangements for me.
She has been urging me to go for some time.

In a way I hate to leave Jerusalem, I have so many interests
here. Last night we had another meeting of the Scout Committee
here. Alex Dushkin — you remember him — has decided with
another young man to take 30 boys camping for a month, during
vacation, near Rehoboth, where they will help with the vintage.
There he expects to put into operation my ideas of organization
and ceremonial. It is a wonderful opportunity . . . I think I am
happier today than I have been on any day since I reached Palestine. . . . Much love. . . . Jessie.

Jerusalem, February 20, 1921

. . . A very happy day: We spent the whole day at Miss Szold's
house, walking there at nine in the morning, and back at 7:30.
It is wonderful how much I can walk now! It must be a mile at
least to Miss Szold's house . . . no, more. In the morning, we had
our reading circle there instead of at our house, as usual (Saturday morning) . In the afternoon, Miss Szold had the second of a
series of meetings with Lady Samuel to discuss Jewish questions
in general and Women's questions in particular. . . . Between
meetings, we wandered in the deep grass in the wild part of
Miss Szold's garden, finding numberless wild flowers. The grass
is even greener here than in Ireland (Poor Ireland!)

March 6, 1921

. . . At last I am getting into the kind of work I really like and
need in order to be satisfied. Sophia Berger and I are forming a
troop of girl scouts, averaging 13 years of age, with a nucleus of
11 girls from the orphanage. Yesterday, Saturday, they met here
for the first time at noon. We had planned to go to a little wood
near here, but as the weather was rather unsettled and wet under-
foot, they met in my sitting-room instead. Little Nancy Samuel,
the 14 year-old daughter of the High Commissioner, also came
to help us. The children seem a bright and interesting group.
As my Hebrew is somewhat superior to Sophia's, I had a little
talk with them, and then Sophia and Nancy went for a long walk
with them around the walls of the Old City, and played games
with them. At about 3:30 Sophia and Nancy returned and had
tea with Deborah and me. . . . Next time we hope to go to the
wood. After that Sophia will take them for outings every Saturday, and I expect to have a meeting and a drawing lesson with
them once during the week. Deborah is giving me rather inten-

sive work in the drawing, and she says I am ready to begin to teach.

I am very well this winter, and evidently this climate suits my bones. Lately I can walk long distances without being tired at all and I can eat practically everything. . . . I thank Mrs. Eder for much of my good health. How I wish I could talk to you about that and many other things!

In her often quoted autobiography Jessie takes stock of her first years in Palestine, of their light and their shadows; and she adds her own projects and some of her plans for the future of the country. She condenses all these thoughts in a fictional letter to an American friend whom she calls Sonya.

Jerusalem, May 25, 1921

Dear Sonya,

I have had a day-dream so satisfying and consoling that I am moved to share it. I want this day-dream to become a reality, that could save us. And I cannot make it nor help to make it a reality except in this way by writing it to you, who, of all persons I know, may be best able to reach those and to cooperate with those who could live out this day-dream.

How far have you over there, working on Jewish problems . . . how far have you realized the disillusionment that eats the heart of every Zionist who comes to live in Palestine? I could never again live anywhere else than in this blessed, beloved land of mine! And yet life here is bitter, bitter! I live now with my feet on earth; I have seen reality; I love it more than my dead iridescent dreams. And yet it is terrible.

The dream of Zionism — as we dreamed it in America — was the dream of a regenerate humanity. The Jewish nation in Palestine was to be not only another nation, but a distinctive nation, to bring salvation amid the orgy of injustice and violence. It was to be our experiment in righteousness. More than that — we would find God again, in the land where He first set His name; find Him not only in ceremonies and prayers but in a way of life that would praise Him with its fullness. We would begin at once. Even now, we thought to catch echoes of a new message. . . .

I came (to Palestine). I shall not review here what I found. . . . I am too impatient to reach the solution, my day-dream. For who knows what day one may die? If I write this you may guess that I want to finish my task and be released. . . . I write not in despair, but in weariness of one who wants to pass on his plow to others.

I found a small Jewish community, so divided in its composition as not to be a community at all — in the sense of having a common spirit — but only an aggregation of individuals. One thing it had in common, a sense of its own dignity and Jewishness, which had strengthened recently, through the settlement of the nationalist groups. To my astonishment, I found this consciousness irritated into chauvinism, partly by insults, repressions and persecutions of that British administration sent by the British Empire pledged to the development of a Jewish homeland. Almost the first thing I heard when I reached Palestine was the indignant outcry over the prohibition to sing Hatikvah, our national air, at public meetings.

A demoralized people, weakened by the destandardization and charities of war, a despairful people, trusting in princes and tricked in its exaggerated hopes, a soulless people, which had substituted expedience for faith and found faithlessness inexpedient.

I came to Jerusalem just before the Holy Days in the fall of 1919. I could not worship in Jerusalem — not with my people. In the synagogues, women are relegated to such undignified seclusion, in a mean room railed off from the congregation, that noble service is impossible. And only the antiquated, railed off from life, visit the synagogue. As for the modern Jews, the intellectuals from Russia, they worship only their own intellects. I understand their psychology of revolt that shatters the pure spirit with the distorted form.

I tried to draw together a small group of persons with a common faith and standard — we might form a nucleus for a future community.

I made two attempts to organize a group. Both failed. . . . I talked myself hoarse.

During the past year, thousands of brave, young, purposeful pioneers came to our land — boys and girls. . . . They planted trees, they raised cabbages and potatoes. We were inadequate. Many found no work, suffered, even died. . . . But nothing could dim those boys and girls.

These, in their life on the land, may rediscover the living faith. What if they have no formal Sabbath, no named God but Labor? Labor is service, and common Labor performed with reverence is the spring of faith, of praise.

You know the climacteric changes of this year, the false despair after the Arab riots of 1920, the false joy after the San Remo decision . . . which promised us the Mandate that is not yet signed, the coming of a Jewish High Commissioner to Palestine with all its romantic and almost religious glamor. And now, when all seemed secure, these new riots, fiercer than the first, our own High Commissioner preventing Jewish immigration, sending back shipfuls of immigrants. . . . Will Great Britain desert us or not?

And then, on a day of sorrow and illness, the day-dream came to me.

From America, which still dreams childish dreams, from such Jews as you, who are Communist as well as Zionist, and who nevertheless also trust in God. . . .

The pioneering conditions here have been likened to pioneer days in North America. The spirit is the same, even though its manifestations be different. The Jewish spirit is to be reborn, it must spring from a consecrated group, not from a debating society, not from a prophet, not from a new synagogue, but from a small group giving their lives for their dream. The great leader must come at last, but we dare not sit still and wait for him. Now, while we have light, we must do what we can to prepare the way. . . .

Let a small group of Jews, ten or twenty families, like-minded in the basic things of life, found a colony and live out their convictions. Let them seek a spot near a Fellahin village of about the same size, and let these two villages for Arabs and for Jews become a model and a symbol in our land. . . .

X

A Book — and a Decision

Wild-berry eyes in a shy brown face,
Under a kerchief of red and brown,
Straight brown legs alive with grace
Under her straight red rag of a gown,
Ran beside me as I looked down,
Answered my greeting and answered my
    speech
In a running Arabic tongue of her own.
But yet we were Jews, speaking each to
    each.
                                    Ballatta

In 1921, something very exciting happened to Jessie Sampter: she again began to write a book; not only the articles which she evidently thought of rather as a duty than as a realization of her own artistic aims, but a book. During the next months, she again and again apologized for her short letters. Soon this "rush of work" would be over; she absolutely wanted to finish the book before the Eders left for Europe, as she very much appreciated Edith's helpful criticism. So far, Mrs. Eder and Leah Berlin were enthusiastic about her book. "If you continue to write like this, you will have written a great book" Edith had told her, after reading the first chapters. In July, 1921, Jessie gave herself another three or four weeks in which to finish. On July 31, 1921, she was still at it, but she was in the midst of the next to the last chapter, and the last would be a shorter one. "So two weeks should finish it."

What book was this, which evidently was finished in its first draft in 1921, but then laid aside and finally revised and revised until almost the day of her death in 1938? Jessie may be her own interpreter, for on August 7, 1921, she wrote:

> Tomorrow — or at the latest — Monday, I shall finish the first draught of my book, and then shall have only revision to do. . . . You warn me not to rush into print. Do you know what I have written? My own story, the story of my life, and I do not even think of having it published while I am alive, now that I have finished it. But I certainly do wish that it shall be published some day.

Even after her own report, it is difficult to settle the question of the book satisfactorily. There are, in fact, two manuscripts which might be meant here. Perhaps she was referring to *The Speaking Heart*. This manuscript, written on very thin paper and revised again and again, is by far the most eloquent account of her first years in Palestine, and so it has been cited extensively. It was never published, and I was fortunate enough to be able to read the second part through the courtesy of Jessie's sister. But there is a second book which answers Jessie's description of its contents. This is the manuscript which kept Jessie busy for more than ten years and which she sent to America, in the last year of her life (1938), very carefully wrapped in sheets. She valued it so highly that she asked her sister to cable her as soon as it arrived. This book is called *In the Beginning* and is also largely autobiographical, as those who have read it claim. Perhaps this book, too, will be published in the near future and give the best account of Jessie's "Beginning."

In 1921, she intended, as she wrote in her next letter, "to lay it away in a drawer for several months, when I may revise it again and have it typewritten." Now, of course, the terrific strain of her breathless work made itself felt. She knew full well that she needed a complete rest and change, and she hoped to find both of these in a stay in Safed, the mountain town which we know so well today as one of the loveliest and most picturesque places in Palestine and also as the place of a new Hadassah lung hospital. But on August 21, 1921, Jessie evidently surprised Elvie by another piece of "great news"; she had decided to come to the States for a while, and in this decision revealed much of what she had until then carefully hidden from her anxious sister in order not to worry her.

> August 21, 1921
>
> . . . . Now I have great news to tell you, and I hope it will make you glad. I have decided to go back to you for a while, as soon as I can make my arrangements and get a steamer. It has not been so sudden a decision as this writing may indicate; for months I have been debating with myself — and with some of my close friends — what I should do, and at last I have come to this conclusion.
>
> You may remember that when I left America with Dr. B.'s (Blumgart's) blessing, so to speak, he said to me: "Go; and if you are not well, come back and I will fix you up." Well, now I am coming back to be "fixed up." I do not for a moment regret, now that I came here and have had these two years now, with all their good and their bad, but I am not certain that it would not have been wiser to get "fixed up" before I left and have come a few months later.
>
> The fact is, I am suffering from great mental depression, which I do not seem to be able to fight off, and which — as you would guess — is affecting my physical health so that I have no strength or energy. Mrs. Eder has helped me as much as she could under the circumstances — the circumstances being short periods of stay in Palestine and those crowded with hard political work and terrible problems. Now she is returning to England for several months. . . . She wanted me to go to Europe, perhaps to Dr. Freud — but if I leave Palestine at all, I must go to you. Sometimes I feel as if only being with you for a while could heal me. . . . So I am coming.
>
> Sometimes I am almost terrified at the idea of not being able to return here; but you helped me so much the first time, I have confidence that you would help me even more, if necessary. For my heart is bound up with this land. It is hard to explain how it holds me, and how, with all my longing to see you, I sometimes feel as if I could not leave it.

VISIT TO AMERICA

From the time Jessie wrote that she had decided to come
back to her sister for a visit, all her letters are full of mixed
feelings: a longing to see her sister . . . "the more I think of it,
the more I long to see you." and a half-suppressed fear that she
would never come back to her beloved Palestine. In between,
she takes time out to explain to Elvie her own special brand
of Zionism and the "split" in the Zionist movement, the
famous split between East and West, between Brandeis and
Weizmann, which was widely discussed in America at that
time.

Jerusalem, July 9, 1921

Dearest Sister,

. . . It is so utterly impossible to write the things I would say!
I am so in the habit of writing you only the pleasant and happy
things — because I don't see why you should share the troubles
I have to lay upon myself — that I have come to avoid writing
at all about the others. Yes, I have suffered very much from the
crisis in Zionist affairs — which is in its last analysis the same as
the world crisis due to the war — and that crisis is not a new
thing. It is much older than the present break in the Organization. In the American affair, I am wholly on the side of
Brandeis, Mack and company — I am writing a letter tonight to
Justice Brandeis to express my confidence — and the others in
America whom you mention I can only think of as acting under
a delusion.

If the Jews in America would stop talking theories and "isms"
and see the practical issues at stake here, the situation would be
saved indeed. The chief difference between the two factions is
one of business method.

You say something about "Nationalism" and "Internationalism." That is very interesting for parlor discussions, but when
one comes to reality and the bitterness of life as one faces it
here, it makes little difference. I, too, am an Internationalist,
and always have been, as I think I explained to you before; but
even the most rabid Internationalist has to live somewhere; he
cannot live everywhere at once. The question Zionism poses is
simply this: Do you want to live a healthy, normal, free life in
Palestine? Or, if you do not, do you want a section of the Jewish
people to have a chance to do it? And as one answers those

questions, one acts — if one is in the habit of paying for one's
convictions.

I must be honest at last, dear; the truth always tells itself at
last. I have suffered almost intolerably, both physically and
mentally in the two years I am here. And yet I never for a
moment regretted my coming. I should do it again — and I have
no intention of leaving. I always told you the truth, but never
the whole truth.

I am telling it now, however, in the book I am writing; I am
telling the whole story of my life, for, curiously, these last years
seem to have made it a story that must be told, a story that
reflects many impersonal matters and insists on being told. How
shall I publish it? And how can I not publish it? I seem to have
come to a deadlock with myself. Let me know how it seems
to you.

Remember, dear, I am satisfied with my own way of life,
despite all its mistakes. I have chosen it and am responsible for
it and shall not regret it no matter what happens. For you to
worry too much about me, is not fair to me. Nevertheless, I
love you to love me even if it is by worrying!

Jerusalem, July 9, 1921

. . . . Sister dear, here's a second letter for today! I just received
yours of June 30, in which you ask me about conditions here
and the split in the Zionist movement. I hope to see you soon,
but I want to answer now. As to the split, there is wrong on both
sides — as in the war — but the far greater wrong on the Weizmann side. And it was they who caused the split, an unpardon-
able sin in this time of crisis. I am sick of all politics, of all
propaganda, and I believe Zionist politics — as all politics — is a
failure. BUT ZIONISM IS NOT AND CANNOT BE A
FAILURE. Just now we are going through a fearful crisis, suffering in part for our own sins, in greater part for the sins of the
world, but I am certain we shall win out. A people that has
suffered persecution for its national ideal for two thousand years,
is not easily discouraged. Your letter makes me glad I am return-
ing to America; perhaps after I regain my strength I can correct
some misconceptions there.

But I am bringing my book, and everything is written in that
for you to read — many things that will surprise you.

So you, too, have been disillusioned, in comfortable New
Rochelle? I thought only Palestine made one wise. I have not
the individual happiness which you can fall back upon; my
personal life has long been a negative quantity.

That is why I cannot escape from this terrible world into my own nest, why I am broken and have to come back to you to be healed.

But I mean to be mended and to fight so long as there is an inch of fight left in me, even if I cannot help to mend the world. I have got that much courage again since I have resolved to break away and make another effort. I confess — before that I had almost lost it for myself.

Lehitraot! Which means: *Auf Wiedersehen* in Hebrew.
Much love from   JESS.

Everything seemed to go according to plan. She had "wonderful luck," as it seemed to Jessie herself. She was able to go with the Eders as far as Egypt; and on August 24, she writes from Cairo, overjoyed, "Here I am on my way already, and I only fear that I may reach you before these letters have had a chance to announce my coming."

Her fear proved justified, it seems. For Elvie, not being notified of Jessie's quick decision, had given the room in her house destined to be "Auntie's room" to a young teacher, Miss James, and Jessie hated to have to get rid of her. Through Elvie's ingenuity, however, it was possible to put up both Jessie and the young teacher, who, after some time, became a good friend of all the family. "Miss Jimmie" frequently appears in Jessie's letters.

Jessie's visit to America in 1921 seems, in general, to have been accompanied by a series of unexpected happenings which after all turned out for the best. The psychoanalyst, for instance, who had promised to "fix her up," if she would want it, was not in New York at the time of her return. She had to go to another psychoanalyst, Dr. Stern, who fortunately turned out to be exactly the sort of physician she needed. He succeeded in finishing the work of the Eders, who had had to leave Palestine before Jessie's analysis was completed. It was Dr. Stern who, at long last, freed her from the traumatic experiences which even in Palestine had continued to burden her mind. From now on she saw in psychoanalysis something like a new priestly craft. She went so far as to write that, if the leading statesmen had been psychoanalyzed before the War, much of the bitterness which had led to the war might have been avoided.

This visit to her sister once more confirmed her own conviction that her place was in Palestine "where I ought to be now, and want to be and hope to be soon," as she wrote in her message to American Youth in the *New Palestine,* (June 23, 1922). On her return to Palestine, Jessie took all of her belongings — eight cases of books and several trunks — as her sister well remembers. For now Jessie knew what she had hoped to see, but only dimly imagined in 1919, when she first came to Palestine. In spite of all her disappointments and worries; here was the land where she wanted to live, not only because of its surpassing beauty and because the climate benefited her health, but because she found so much to do, and because she wanted to share the immense task of rebuilding the ancient homeland of her people.

RETURN TO PALESTINE

Jessie left America in October, 1922, in the company of Eve Dushkin, a member of the friendly family whom she had known so well in Jerusalem. She felt rather proud of her own decision to go by "second cabin" this time: "The differences, except a feeling of superiority, are not worth paying for (and that I have anyhow!)" she commented cheerfully and characteristically.

But this courage and stamina had to prove themselves during this trip. Even a good sailor like Jessie had to confess that this time they had a "real storm as bad as any she had ever experienced before . . . or even a little worse," as she adds cheerfully. With a sort of grim humor she describes how a giant wave flooded the deck before they were warned to go inside, and how the dishes slid from side to side on the table. Her reaction shows how rested and refreshed she felt now. Her own and Mrs. Eder's remedy, the visit to her sister, had evidently "healed her." In fact, the reader of her letters cannot help the heretical feeling that the long-missed companionship of her sister may have done more for her than all her psychoanalysis.

Once the Palestine customs formalities had been passed, the first impressions after her return were happy ones. Miss Szold, Leah Berlin and Miss Berger, Henrietta Szold's friend and secretary, were at the boat to welcome her, and the "home" which she now shared with Leah's mother, old Mrs. Berlin, and Leah's twin brother and sister gave her much contentment. Above all, the conditions in Palestine seemed more congenial than before. It is true that the financial crisis was as bad as ever; there were teachers who had not seen any salary for six months — and still went on teaching. All her friends told her how well she looked; some people even called her "fat" — a slight exaggeration, it would seem to anyone familiar with her pictures. Anyhow, she felt gratified to know that her friends thought her "good-looking" — and she duly reported it to her sister.

TAMAR

All this regained strength of body and soul gave her the courage to realize a long cherished plan. In Jerusalem, when she had been sick, Yemenite children from the Orphanage had come to see her and bring her flowers. Ever since then she had dreamed one dream: why not take one of these little girls into her own home and make her feel that she was loved as a daughter is loved by her own mother?

She did not lose much time before she began to realize her plan. She came back in October, 1922; as early as November, she writes that she "begins to look for a little girl whom I want to befriend."

Jerusalem, November 17, 1922.
. . . The other day, I saw a little girl, in whom I am going to
interest myself — (with a view to adoption?). She is a darling,
with dark curls and big appealing black eyes. She's not quite
three; was found in a basket hanging on a tree during the
blizzard here, three days old. There was a Hebrew label saying
that her name was Tamar, which means Palmtree . . .

The reader may remember the little girl who was born
during the blizzard in 1921 and was left in the snow. Then
the nurses used to call her Tamar Sheleg; now she became
Tamar Sampter and the "miracle" which brought to Jessie
Sampter's lonely heart all the joys and cares of motherhood
that life had denied her. At first, Tamar seemed a very nervous,
frightened child, as other observers have told us and as Jessie's
own letters concede; every second word of hers was "I am
afraid." Moreover, little Tamar was taciturn and repressed
to a degree that made some people think her not quite normal.
It was all the more exciting for a born educator like Jessie to
change the child and transform a high-strung, nervous being
into a healthy, normal child. "Whoever saves one soul, has
saved one world" our sages said. In that case, if Jessie Sampter
had done nothing else but saved the soul of one unhappy baby,
she would have earned her share in the world to come.

Of course, Jessie, trained in modern child-psychology, did
not underestimate the responsibility which she took upon herself in adopting a child of unknown origin. Not only did she
have the physicians at the orphanage test Tamar physically
before she took her into her own home, so as to make sure
that she was an absolutely healthy child, she also had her in-
telligence examined by the tests which she asked her sister to
send her. Both tests proved Tamar to have the average reac-
tions of a three-year old child; in fact, she seemed slightly
above average. That Jessie Sampter did not act on sudden
impulse in taking on her new responsibility is obvious, but in
the end, as in all important decisions of her life, she acted
without asking anybody's advice. In time, she came to con-

sider her little daughter as a bond between herself and America. A close friend of hers had helped her financially to adopt Tamar by sending her a sum of money annually, and all her friends helped by sending clothes and outfits for the little girl. In the end Jessie had to protest; she did not want her little "country girl" to be dressed like a society belle.

Jessie's letters in those years are almost a practical study of child psychology; her principal aim was to make the child independent, not only of life's external conditions, but also of her own care. After devoting most of her time to Tamar in the first months of the child's stay in her home, she gradually withdrew in order to free her from overmuch clinging to her new "Imma," as Tamar "thrillingly" called the woman whom, before, she had only known as *"geveret* Sampter." Some samples from Jessie's letters may serve to reveal both her delight in her little daughter and her sober appreciation of the child's abilities:

On January 24, 1924, Jessie wrote to her sister:

> I am having a great daily joy in Tamar now, not only because she is intelligent and sweet . . . and sometimes tantalizing . . . and healthy and happy, but because of the change that has taken place in her in this half year and is still proceeding. She came to me as a timid nervous child. Every second word was "I'm afraid." Now I have not heard the word in months. She has changed from a child that faced life with suspicion and misery to one who faces it with confidence and joy. To do so much for a baby's soul is worth while, no matter what comes afterwards. And I love her so much, that I am often afraid, as mothers always are. . . .

> January 14, 1925.
> . . . I study my own little daughter with much interest. She is certainly not stupid, she has a good receptive intelligence and common sense. But she is not what I consider the creative or imaginative type. Though she plays beautifully alone with her dolls, etc., she has no imaginary playmates, she does not invent stories or songs, though she repeats them well. . . . She is very loving and loyal and reacts properly and quickly to all social appeals. I expect her to be a trained nurse or farmerette, or some such other useful practical sort of person. . . .

MOVING TO REHOBOTH

In all her happiness with her new little daughter, Jessie did not forget that Palestine needed her; and her own special task, the Yemenite work, claimed her more and more. It was with the thought of these two activities in mind, care for Tamar and care for the Yemenites, that she decided to move from Jerusalem to Rehoboth in 1924. She felt that it was better for a child to grow up amidst orange groves and vineyards than in a big city, and as we mentioned before, there was, in Rehoboth, a large colony of Yemenites with whom she wanted to get better acquainted.

In February, 1924, her friend, the engineer, Boris Kazmann, and his sister came to see her in Jerusalem. They were living in Rehoboth, and it was this visit which moved her to go there. On February 20, she excitedly writes to her sister:

> Jerusalem, February 20, 1924.
> ... I am quite excited and really very happy over a decision I have made this week. ... I have decided not only to move to new and larger quarters but to move away from Jerusalem altogether and settle in the country. It is by no means a new decision or a new idea — I have been thinking about it for years — but of course a decision is always sudden when one finally takes it.
> I am going to Rehoboth. It is by common consent the most beautiful and healthful of all the Jewish settlements. Rehoboth is — with its rolling hills, its vineyards, orange and almond orchards and grove of eucalyptus trees — very lovely, with sweeping views on the west to the white sand dunes that just hide the Mediterranean and on the east to the mountain range that hides Jerusalem. And the village itself is so charming — with its neat little white houses clustered among trees and flower gardens. I know several of the people there — besides Boris Kazmann and his sister whose coming helped to decide me — and I like them. Among them are two well-known writers, Aharoni, the zoologist and ornithologist of Palestine, and the Kindergartner, who is perhaps the best in Palestine, is a very interesting woman. I went down for two days this week to see what possibilities there are for renting houses and I was very pleasantly surprised. I saw two which I like so much that it is hard to decide which I want. In both I shall get four rooms for what I am now paying for

two, with good kitchen, garden and porch. I can keep chickens
and a cow and become a farmer if I like — though I think I shall
wait a bit to increase my family . . . and Shulamith* is very
pleased to go with me. By the way, the longer I have her, the
more I like her. I call her my elder daughter — she will be twenty
tomorrow . . . and I think she also feels that we belong together,
though she is not yet here two months. I hope to get her a
husband in Rehoboth — like all mothers. . . .

No sooner said than done. On March 10, not more than two
weeks later, Jessie was happy and busy "getting her house in
order" in Rehoboth. She had been lucky in finding a house
very conveniently situated, next door to the *Beth Haam,* the
People's House, where all the lectures and concerts were held,
and quite near to the kindergarten which Tamar was attending
for the first time when Jessie wrote this letter.

"On the whole, I am very happy, and very comfortable, despite
some of the difficulties of getting settled. And I confess it is
partly the desire to be and feel permanently well that has driven
me to this quiet, healthful place. I am tired of getting tired, and
I really, selfishly want to enjoy living.
P.S. Do I sound happy or not? I'm too busy and too vividly
living to be able to judge myself.

J.

Later on, she confessed to her sister that right at present she
did not want to write prose at all, only to live and work. . . .

"Yet I have already written several poems since I am here.
Indeed, singing, whether silently or not, seems to be the only
spiritual exercise for which I have any taste just now . . . and
probably the silent songs do less damage. . . ."

Strange, almost prophetic words: "Singing" was the task re-
quired in the near future from Jessie Sampter. But it was
neither a person nor an idea which moved her to sing. It was
the Land itself which awakened her song. She discovered the
Emek, the Valley of the Children, as she preferred to call it,
and about it she wrote her most significant book.

---

* Shulamith, her faithful maid, a Yemenite girl.

XI

The Song of the Emek

This is the Valley of the Children,
This is the way the singing children go,
Westwards and upwards towards a rising
sun.
Freedom and work — the gift our children
ask —
Freedom and work — the gift our land has
given —
Are calling us, prophetic voices calling
To the beginning at the end of days:
The Emek

In the midst of her busy, quiet life in Rehoboth, Jessie quite unexpectedly received a request from the Jewish National Fund (J.N.F.) to tour the Valley of Jezreel. This trip was primarily intended to furnish material for a series of articles for the *New Palestine,* the periodical in which Jessie's articles were published ever since its beginning in 1923; but this excursion proved to be an overwhelming experience for her, keenly interested in social experiments as she was. Eventually, it became the inspiration for her lovely *The Emek.*

On March 8, 1925, she wrote to her sister from Nahalal (in the Valley of Jezreel):

> As usual, I decided at a moment's notice when to take my trip; and I didn't write you that I was considering it. This is the trip for the Jewish National Fund, and I shall probably be away for another three weeks. I'll write you details later, and most of what I write will be in articles, not letters.

Jessie herself did not quite know what was going to happen to her in the three weeks that lay ahead. Luckily, we are in a position to follow her footsteps rather closely and watch how the new impressions took hold of her. It is true that the Jewish National Fund had made the extended trip possible, because its sponsors wanted a first-hand report on the life of the young men and women, most of them college-bred, who with "black labor" were working the land and building the villages in the Valley of Jezreel. But neither the Jewish National Fund nor Jessie herself had any idea how the discovery of this new world, men and scenery and social enterprise, would impress the soul of a poet who was at the same time a social reformer and had been anxiously waiting for an expirement like this. Fortunately, her letters to Mr. Weisgal, the Editor of *New Palestine,* have been made available, and they offer a spectacle of rare psychological and biographical interest.

ARTICLES THAT TURNED INTO POEMS

Jessie, as we have already mentioned, had been writing monthly articles for the *New Palestine* ever since its inception in 1922. So she evidently started to write an article about the Emek, too; but she had to discover that "the Emek *sings itself.*" Rarely are we allowed to look as closely into the workshop of a poet as at this time in 1925, when a frail woman, hampered by various attacks of influenza, took this trip.

It all began with her letter to Mr. Weisgal, on April 16, 1923, from Rehoboth:

Dear Mr. Weisgal,
I have not written anything for you in two months, because I was away from home on an extended trip through the Emek and Jordan Valley to visit the workingmen's groups there. I shall send you articles on these settlements at intervals of a few weeks, to make up for lost time. The trip was planned by the J.N.F., and they ask that they be permitted to publish any of the articles they may wish simultaneously with you. . . . I take it for

granted that you have no objection to this. The J.N.F. defrayed
my traveling expenses, but they are of course not paying for
my work. . . .
    P.S. This was again delayed by an attack of influenza.

In this letter Jessie still speaks of "articles" which she is plan
ning, but the story looks different to her on May 17:

                                                          May 17, 1925
    Dear Mr. Weisgal,
        I am still on the convalescent list, and though I am hard at
    work on a serious piece of writing on the Emek, I haven't finished
    it yet. . . . I am writing a series of pictures on the Emek, which
    are not exactly prose and yet I hope not too much poetry for the
    practical *New Palestine*. I am doing as I must; the Emek sings
    itself. It is much more wonderful than anything one can say
    about it.
        What did you do with my Halutz songs?

On May 31, she is still uncertain about the fate of her Emek
sketches.

                                                          May 31, 1925.
    . . . You will call me the *enfant terrible* of your contributors,
    when you see that I am again sending you something that looks
    like poetry. The fact is, I had intended writing "articles" about
    the Emek. During the delay, due to influenza, I realized, how-
    ever, that I could write about it only in this form . . . call it
    poetry, prose or any other name that smells as sweet . . . and I
    am writing a series of these pictures which I hope may later
    form a book. I hope, too, that being an editor with imagination,
    you will decide to publish them. If so, would it be worth while
    holding the type for book use or not? I only suggest it. . . . In case
    you decide against using this series on the Emek, I shall have to
    stop writing for you for a few months, that is, until I finish it,
    as I find I cannot do any other creative work at the same time.
    I hope to make up later. And I sincerely hope you use it. Note
    that *it tells in briefer form the same tale as an article, and it tells
    what has not been told before.*
        Yours with friendly greetings,
                                                          JESSIE E. SAMPTER

Mr. Weisgal, being as she called him "an editor with imagination," seems to have lived up to her expectations. Without

Jessie E. Sampter, September 14, 1925

any further delay, he sent her an issue of the *New Palestine* containing the first of her poems on "The Emek." We readily understand why he added: "No further comment is necessary." On June 17, the delighted author replied:

> Dear Mr. Weisgal,
> I was equally delighted with your letter about my series on the Emek, and the copies of the *New Palestine* containing it, both of which reached me by the same mail. I am sending you herewith the third installment. . . . On the very day . . . yesterday . . . on which I received your letter, I had finished the series, so that I need only copy and send it to you. . . . I have no objection to you breaking them up into still smaller sections, provided you leave nothing out. I am very glad you are holding the type. . . . I shall later write you my plans about book publication. I hope to call it not *The Emek* but *The Valley of the Children.* I hope you have received safely the second installment, *Batya,* and also my letter about the Youth Movement. . . .

So we gather from these reports from the poet's workshop, that in spite of several attacks of influenza, perhaps because of the enforced rest and the chance to ponder on these poems, Jessie composed the main poems in the short period between April 16, when she still was planning some "articles," and May 31, when she confessed to her editor that she was "sending him something that looks like poetry, but that she could only report to him in this form because "The Emek sings itself." Jessie completed the first series on July 16, as we know from her letter to Mr. Weisgal of July 17. Several years later it was published in book form, and Jessie's sister, had the not-quite-easy mission of corresponding with the publisher; for Jessie, who returned to the United States in 1925-26, had had to undergo a major operation, and was unable to prepare the' book-edition as she had planned to do.

The slender little book contains fifteen "prose-poems" as the contemporaries would have called them, sketches of the different settlements and their problems. They are as vivid today as they were in the beginning of the settlements in 1925.

In fact, we shall see that some of the problems which have
come out into the open only in our days (1953) were already
clearly seen and commented upon by this poetic observer.

The edition was sold out; evidently this happened more
rapidly than the publisher anticipated, and one is tempted to
suggest that the little book bears reprinting, as the poems are
as alive today as they were when Jessie felt moved to write
them. It is true that they are influenced by the prose poems
of Walt Whitman which Jessie had read in her youth and liked
very much. But there is another and a more modern echo in
them which brings them nearer to the "new school" of poetry
that only came into being in America while Jessie was far
away in Palestine. Like Edgar Lee Masters, in his *Spoon River
Anthology,* Jessie here gives us clearly-seen profiles of men and
women. But these Emek sketches are unique in showing her
ability to combine the scenic background with the portraits
of the working-men and women and their problems. For the
author's ultimate intention was to depict the problems of the
working youth in Palestine. This comes out clearly in the
Prologue and Epilogue which Jessie added to the book.

The Prologue reads as follows:

> "I went home to the Emek
> I rode alone through the fields and the groves
> But everywhere I came, hands were waved to greet me
> Hands stretched forth to meet me and draw me in."

The Epilogue reads:

> "This is the Valley of the Children,
> Westwards and upwards towards a rising sun.
> Freedom and work — the gift our children ask —
> Freedom and work — the gift our land has given —
> Are calling us, prophetic voices calling
> To the beginning at the end of days."

VIGNETTES OF EMEK CHARACTERS

The Emek evidently was something new for the author as well as for the reader. Like the giants of olden times the simple heroes rise up out of the ground; each one of them is an Antaeus, whose strength is reborn out of his return to his mother Earth. But let the different sketches speak for themselves. There is "Regeneration," about the lone farm-woman of Nahalal. Everybody knows her and calls her by her first name, the name which she gave herself to signify the essence of her being. She had lost her betrothed when he was shot through the heart "defending an outpost against Bedouins," and now she is living all alone, tending her cows and poultry alone, working her ground alone. She is a homely woman now and two teeth are missing; but twenty years ago, when she came to the land "she was a girl of alabaster, white-handed and thin." In spite of all her hard work she is not unhappy now; there are flowers on her table for Shabbat, she offers you bread of her own wheat, her eggs, her butter, her cheese. "She eats the work of her hands." The country has saved her, she does not feel lonely now. "Here is the regeneration of the sacred earth." She represents the "veterans" among the *halutzot,* the pioneering women of Palestine.

But there is youth right behind her to take up the tools should her old hands weaken: Ben Brak, the son of the lightning, shaggy and tall, and his blue-eyed young wife with their little son. Most important of all, there are the children who grow up in the country. Their teachers teach them in a bare room "with a few paints and pencils," but in a way which sophisticated psychologists of New York and London might envy. For the land teaches them, along with the educators. Here they have invented a school which "not only pours words into molds of knowledge," but educates character, will and mind. The children themselves tell how gladly they work with

their hands, making chairs, feeding chickens, growing vegetables. They learn to make, to create something, just as the
grown-ups do.

But the open-eyed author does not limit herself to admiring
their success; she also notes and discusses their problems. The
problems of boy and girl in the *Kevutzah*, the problem of East
and West. The *Hasidim* in their skullcaps and long beards
seem worlds apart from the "Young Watchmen" (Hashomer
Hazair) whose religion is embodied in his work for the earth,
the rebuilding of the land. However, Jessie does not find these
two worlds incompatible. On Passover, the *Yablona Hasidim*
visit the farmers of Nahalel and "Jewish hands stretched out
across the grass. . . ."

Not all of this charming little book is given up to heroic
stories of the first settlers; there is a pungent grain of satire
added, when the author watches the tourists both Gentile and
Jewish, who come to Palestine. Both are equally far from understanding the essence of the Palestine endeavor. The Gentile
tourists come to the Land "begloved and begoggled and be-
camera-ed." Their auto is waiting . . . while

> "They walk adventurously, carrying a dainty lunch in
>   napkins and wax paper
> To eat and drink at Gideon's soldiers well.
> They look suspiciously
> At this village, full of Hebrew speaking rabble,
>   barefooted and slackly clad.
> They greet with nose-stopped condescension the
>   shoemaker, a young and bearded Jew . . .
> It's good they had not time to visit
> The carpenter. They might have turned their noses
>   Up at Jesus."

But the Jewish tourists are not much more understanding:

They cannot understand why the young settlers stay in this austere country:

> "In summer they burn and in winter they freeze
> Then why do they come and why do they stay?
>
> . . . . .
>
> Don't you long for Fifth Avenue, pine for Broadway?
> Don't you long for a bath in a white porcelain room?
> Can they stand these discomforts, this pricking and
>   sticking?
> Just camping at night and just working by day?
> Then why do they come and why do they stay?"

This certainly seems like an echo of all the tourists' criticisms which Jessie must have heard from the Americans who came in those years because "it was the thing to do.

XII

Building Her Own House in Rehoboth

Out of the earth and rocks
Out of the land and sea,
The brothers of my flesh and blood
Have made a house for me.
Of earth and rocks and sand
It lifts its airy tower;
And they are like its gardeners,
That tend a growing flower.
Mine was the seed, the dream,
The urging of desire;
But while I sit and sing to them
The walls grow higher, higher. . . .
My House

The year of her tour through Emek Yizreel, the "Valley of the Children," as she liked to call it, had started most pleasantly for Jessie. Her own distillation of her impressions in her prose-poetry sketches a new form of society newer than she dared confess at this time; here for the first time she had the chance to observe a "moneyless and classless society" which had been her dream of the society of the future and which in the last years of her life she found realized in the *kevutzah* of Givat Brenner. With a view to preparing these entirely novel sketches for publication in book form, the *New Palestine* had held the type; and so Jessie cheerfully went back to see her sister and her American friends in 1925-26, in order to take care of this new book of poetry herself.

But the trip turned out differently. Once she was in America, it was discovered that the frequent ailments from which she had suffered during the first years in Palestine were not due to a nervous condition but had a physiological origin. A serious operation was needed; a fibroid growth had to be removed. The operation was performed and left Jessie rather weak, as was to be expected, but she longed "to go home". And that's what she did, though often in the coming years she would mention in her letters that perhaps it would have been better to have stayed a little longer in New Rochelle and to have given herself time to recuperate. At the time, though, Jessie's longing for the homeland and for the little girl who was waiting for her in Rehoboth, prevailed, and so she sailed in January, 1926, on the Roma.

On Shipboard

On the whole, it was a pleasant trip and full of quaint adventures which testify to the singular appeal that this shy woman had for many people of different backgrounds. There was a young man from the Azores who came and told her all sorts of interesting details about the cultural and social backwardness of those charming islands, for he had "taken a funny liking to her," as she smilingly wrote to her sister. And there was a meeting with an extraordinary woman, a descendant of the Marranos in Portugal, the Jews who had been compelled to give up their ancient faith in time of persecution.

But the most thrilling adventure of all was the meeting with about 800 young immigrants to Palestine. Of course, they traveled third class, these boys and girls; they were splendid young people from the "Young Watchman" (Hashomer Hatzair), and Jessie felt that it was "good to know that so many of that type are coming!"

When she arrived, her good friend and neighbor from Rehoboth, Boris Kazmann, was at the pier to welcome her. That was a blessing, for the landing proved to be a great strain, as any landing is. Moreover, she caught a cold and had to stay in bed for a few days. But in spite of all that, her homecoming seemed perfect. Slowly, her own life returned "to normalcy." But she still had to go to bed early, and she tired easily. However, she enjoyed eating all sorts of vegetables from her own garden; and her flower garden was her delight, though she still felt too weak to work in it as she liked to do all the days of her life.

HER OWN HOUSE

The next few years were full of a tremendous experience. For a long time Jessie had been wanting to build her own house, for she knew full well that he who builds a house in Palestine helps to build up the land.

All her letters from then on are brimful of this new thrilling enterprise. At first, she seems to have had some trouble with a woman architect who proved incompetent; but at last she found an ideal architect who understood her and built the house which her dreams had shown to her. This house, at 15 Weizmann Street, was destined to be a cultural center as long as Jessie lived in it. Afterwards, it served as a temporary shelter for Dr. and Mrs. Weizmann before they built their own home, and it was gratefully mentioned by Dr. Weizmann in his autobiography.

Of course, the workmen who built her house, had to be "members of the union" according to her socialistic ideas. With a quaint solemnity she told her friends of "laying the cornerstone." At the same time, she wrote her significant poem "My house." This poem was suggested to her by her lifelong friend, an ailing spinster, Miss Alberta Hall, who never in her life had owned a home of her own. She wrote to her:

Rehoboth, February 11, 1926
. . . Did Elvie tell you that I am beginning to build my own house? It is a very exciting and happy experience. I have given

Jessie Sampter, Boris Kazmann and friends in garden of Jessie's house, 1927

over the contract to an engineer, so that I will have no worry whatsoever; I also like him personally. This week we laid the cornerstone ... "we" means Tamar and I ... and although my lot is only about seven minutes' walk from here, I had to take an automobile to go there and carry an easy-chair in the car to sit on there. About thirty or so people came, including the workmen, only the people I know and like the best, at eleven in the morning. I put a sealed bottle into the foundation, containing a parchment relating in Hebrew the date, the occasion and the names of the owners, Tamar and I, and that the house is built by Jewish laborers. Some day, it may be an antiquity. Then Tamar and I each threw in three shovel-fulls of cement ... for the house is of cement, not stone ... and after that everybody had wine (no prohibition here) and cakes. ...

Some weeks later (December 3, 1926) Jessie gave a more elaborate description of the "laying of the cornerstone" to her sister:

Rehoboth, December 3, 1926
... Last Tuesday I laid the cornerstone of my house, and today — Friday — the foundation is finished. I hope to move in by the end of April.

Tuesday was a beautiful sunny day — about like May in New York and although the lot is only seven minutes from here, of course, I had to take an automobile to take me there. Shulamith went early to the lot, to get the party ready, and Tamar, who was excused from school, went to the village "Main Street" to fetch the auto at 10:30. Most of the guests, invited for 11, were there before us. Besides Mr. Theiner, my engineer-constructor, and the 15 workmen, there were only about 15 other persons, just those I care most about and my nearest neighbors. The foundations had all been dug out already, and I could see where each room was going to be. As I walked over the bare ground, prickly with dry thistles, I imagined the lovely garden and trees that I hope to put there. The place is beautiful, high and open without being on a hill. It slopes toward the southwest. On the north, behind Shulamith's lot, there is a vineyard as far as one can see. On the east and west I have neighbors, not very near and not on a line with my own house. My neighbor on the east is Dr. Aharoni, the ornithologist and zoologist of Palestine, connected with the Hebrew University. We are on friendly terms. To the south is the street — or road — and across it the whole village, embowered in green, at my feet, with a view of the

Judaean mountains to the S.E.: B.K.'s back yard, all trees and
vegetables, is almost opposite. It is very rural and lovely, altogether with rolling country on all sides.

I had brought a bottle containing a parchment on which were
written the date, the event, Tamar's and my name, and that the
house was built by Jewish laborers. B.K. sealed it for me with
red sealing wax, and I put it in the corner, Tamar followed up
with three shovel fulls more, and then did not want to stop.
(After all, the house is to be built of cement, not stone. But
more about that later.) After that my guests put in their shovel
fulls, too, and wished me fifty-seven varieties of good wishes.
Then we went to where a table had been spread in the construction shed on Shulamith's part of the lot. We had cookies and
chocolate cakes and heaps of oranges and several kinds of wine —
no prohibition here — and two short and sweet speeches. One
was made by Aharoni, in the name of my new neighbors; all of
whom I invited, in my reply, to my housewarming next May.
The other was made by one of the workingmen, who spoke in
appreciation of the fact that I put in the contract that only labor
union members are to be employed, and in general spoke in a
friendly way, because it is pretty well-known here where one's
sympathies lie.

I was much moved, especially when he said that the workingmen take great satisfaction in each new house that is built in
the country, even though they leave it as they come to it. These
workingmen —— and two girls among them — are chiefly high
school graduates or college students, the pioneers. Most of them
still live in tents, themselves. I answered because I could not help
myself, and I don't know what I said. There is unemployment
here now, and to build is to ease the situation. It is different,
building here, from building elsewhere; it is not only building
a home, but building the country.

"I have never been happier, or shall I say: more happily
occupied and involved in life," Jessie wrote to her sister. "I
am in the midst of the exciting process of building my own
house . . . then, I have a little daughter who is healthy, happy,
and intelligent . . . and besides has one of the sweetest, warm-
est, most generous and yet elusive natures that I have ever
known."

The political situation also seemed to her very satisfactory. The Arabs appeared to be satisfied with the English

policy; it is true, there remained political agitators, but the people were not behind them. On the other hand, the Jewish masses were willing to cooperate with the Arabs. This was one reason why Jessie was so happy and at peace here. "It is at once a haven in the present and a presage of a calmer future."

Cheerfully, Jessie went back to the all-engrossing matter of watching the progress of the workmen who were building her house. In January, 1927, she wrote:

> . . . It seems my house will be ready sooner than I expected. It is finished up to the roof now. I have paid that far.

And on April 20, 1927:

> What is it that makes getting one's own house such a deep delight? I feel almost as I did when Tamar came to me, that a great and wonderful thing is happening. I feel like a snail that has been naked and is acquiring a shell. I wonder how it will be afterwards? I don't imagine the pleasure will ever stale, as far as the house itself is concerned.
>
> As for happiness, it runs in the family, that I have a kind of panicky feeling that it can't last forever, and therefore treasure and value it all the more.
>
> I want you so "awfly" to come out here for a visit. Tamar, being younger than I, is even more impatient.
>
> May 4, 1927.
>
> Today I am moving into my new house, or rather, Shulamith is doing the moving, with plenty of good assistants, and I am having lunch at B. K.'s house and resting there. At about 4 o'clock I shall walk over to the house and get settled. My contractor is here and hung my curtains this morning, he tells me. What do you think of a contractor like this? This afternoon, he tells me, he expects to arrange all my books before I go over, and as he knows English well, he is likely to do it as well as I could. . . . People always take care of me; even Tamar does. I rather need it, as I have not been so well for the last week or two. I don't know why my heart has been misbehaving again. . . .
>
> May 8, 1927
>
> I am in my own house now three days, and I cannot tell you how wonderful it is. . . .

> I am sure my house will make me well. . . . It is so comfortable.
> I can't quite realize it is all mine and I may always stay here.

These letters have been quoted extensively, because, better than any comments, they reveal how childishly happy Jessie felt at the prospect of having her home to herself. Only now did she allow herself to take account of all the discomforts of a rented house: lack of privacy, neighbors who shared bath and toilet but did not share her own ideas on cleanliness, and so on. Of course, like everybody who builds a house, she had some financial worries: the first budget was the minimum, (she knew the danger), and now "the final cost will be only a trifle above her maximum!" But "worry" is too strong a word, in view of all the delight her house afforded her.

One of her most important gains was that now she could take upon herself all the liabilities of a householder in Palestine. In addition, the "little Yemenite girls," her special favorites, who worked in the daytime, could meet in her home in the evenings. Jessie, as we know, had founded a "club" for them, where she and her friends taught them to read and write and discussed with them some of the problems of life. Moreover, her little house soon became "a house on the road," where tourists were always welcome. Jessie considered it one of her duties toward the homeland to interpret its beauties and explain its liabilities to strangers.

Jessie's Writings at Rehoboth

In the midst of all this pleasurable excitement about her new home, a new literary task appeared on the horizon. A new edition of her *Guide to Zionism* was wanted.

> I have been asked to edit a new third edition of the "Guide to Zionism" which is out of print and needed for the student societies. But I shall try to get them to do it in America and let me just help from here. . . . There is very little money and very much work in it; I should not mind that, but, one thing, I want

to work on my novel now, and, another thing, I think it can be
done more quickly and efficiently there. I am very delighted that
it is needed, though.

As we see from her letter, she was not over-enthusiastic about
the prospect though she was, of course, "delighted" that the
book was "needed."

Another literary success came her way. In April, 1927, she
received a cable telling her that she had won the prize in a
poetry contest for the best National Fund song in English,
"The Four Winds." Jessie had assumed the pseudonym,
"Shunamite," which is revealing in itself; she must have felt
like the "Woman of Shunem" in Biblical times who "lived
among her own people." The prize was $100.00, "which be-
side the great moral satisfaction is also extremely welcome at
this juncture." (April 25, 1927).

"I am sometimes ridiculously happy!" Jessie wrote in the
first enthusiasm after moving into her own house; and in July,
1927, she more soberly reiterates this feeling: "I am delighted.
Life is good; my garden is beautiful; my house is very satisfying. I have little troubles and big joys."

Even the earthquake which shook Rehoboth in 1927 could
not frighten her; on the contrary, it seemed to prove to her
that, as it so often happened in her life, she had been at the
very edge of disaster without its even touching her.

CALM BEFORE THE STORM

These years in Rehoboth, in her own house, just preceding
the outbreak of the Arab riots in 1929, were an idyllic interval
in Jessie's dramatic life. It is true, her health was still shaken
by the after-effects of her operation. But she was getting better
from day to day; and by and large, she had never felt so happy
in all her life.

It makes melancholy reading today, in the years of constant
Jewish-Arab clashes and assaults, to see how Jessie in those

years again and again stressed the safety of Jews and Arabs
living peacefully together — two years before the massacre of
the Jewish students in Hebron!

In the background of all this happiness, there certainly was
the feeling in Jessie's heart of hearts that she must not neglect
to work in her own vineyard. She revised her novel and worked
in her flower garden, and her only worries were the financial
difficulties concerning her work with the Yemenites, as shown
in her letters to Dr. Dushkin. In fact, sometimes, in those
years "before the deluge" as we see them now, she could not
overcome a sort of "panicky feeling," as she herself expressed
it, that such happiness could not last forever. In keeping with
her own favorite idea that the present moment was the only
value in life and eternity, she decided to treasure her present
happiness all the more. But to the reader of 1956, her foreboding seems to have something of a prophetic character, soon
to be verified in 1929. Not long afterwards, Jessie's feeling
of "almost delirious happiness" changed to her "Lamentations." The year of disaster was near at hand which was
destined to shatter all her fond dreams of Isaac and Ishmael
living peacefully together.

And Jessie Sampter, after her jubilant songs of men and
women working in the Emek, was destined to sing her lament
"After the Riots:"

> "I heard the twittering birds in the quiet, quiet dawn
> And my soul was like a howling wind that tore them
>   shred to shred
> For in my quiet land of peace the sword of hate is
>   drawn,
> And the quiet and the peaceful are the dead."

XIII

The Fateful Year (1929)

Ishmael, my brother, lift not your hand
    against mine:
Have we not one father? is not this land
    His shrine?
We are one flesh and blood, we have one
    need and hunger,
Ishmael, lift not your hand — I am the
    younger.
            Ishmael, My Brother.

Afte these quiet, busy and deeply contented years of building and planning, it is moving to note that, for once in her life, Jessie did not allow her happiness to be affected by the world-wide and Zionist depression which reigned in those years and which brought about the decrease of the immigrants. The fateful year of 1929 opened with a great joy. At long last, her sister and her brother-in-law came to Palestine in order to learn about all the things which Jessie, in spite of her weekly reports, "had not been able to write:" her own self, her activities, her life in her new little home and, most of all, the country itself.

Jessie looked forward to this visit with anticipation. In her usual practical way, which went along with her poetic vision, she had an extensive tour arranged for them even before they arrived. She herself and Tamar, who was only nine years old at the time, were to accompany their guests as escorts and guides, while a private car took them through a considerable number of the new settlements. So they saw the Valley of Jezreel, the background of Jessie's book, *The Emek;* they also saw many of the *kevutzot* in the country; they even saw Acco, the quaint old Arabic town, with its minarets and its prison, where they had lunch with the friendly warden. From Mrs. Wachenheim's letters one gets the impression that the visitors were not quite as happy with this visit as Jessie herself. They found it all vastly interesting, but uncomfortable. They suffered much from heat and mosquitoes and were glad to sail home.

In August, Jessie and her daughter went to Tel Aviv, that "Soap-Bubble City," which she did not like overmuch because of its "American resort" buildings. Among other things, she planned to give Tamar the pleasure and recreation of sea-bathing. In this she succeeded, and Tamar felt happy and loved her outdoor life with her many friends there. Jessie, however, did not feel very comfortable in the big boarding house in Tel Aviv; she resented the flies and the long dull meals she had to sit through, and she missed her "happy home" in the village. Yet she gladly overlooked all these minor discomforts as long as her stay in Tel Aviv served her major purpose in coming there — her negotiations about the new kindergarten in Rehoboth. She had discovered the ideal kindergartner, Maya Rosenberg, whose name is well-known in Israel today from the Maya Rosenberg Institute in Rehoboth. Not only was this woman a trained psychologist, who "had all the new ideas" which could be used for the benefit of Jessie's Yemenite kindergarten, but she was also eager to establish the kindergarten in Rehoboth, which suited Jessie's plans. It all depended now on getting more funds to buy a house and garden for the kindergarten, which was badly needed. Jessie, who had saved a small sum from her private fund, given to her by American friends in order to provide lunches for her kindergarten, was willing to buy the house and donate it to the Jewish National Fund.

THE ARAB RIOTS

"Otherwise no news," so Jessie ended her letter to her sister on August 22, 1929. In the week of August 23, with the suddenness of lightning, violence struck peaceful Palestine. Among the Moslems, emissaries had circulated arousing the people and warning them to be ready for "the Day." On Friday, the 23rd of August, armed hordes of Arabs flocked to Jerusalem; no attempts were made to disarm them, except at one gate, where the disarming was soon stopped "by government order." In the Mosque area the Grand Mufti addressed the crowds. All this could lead to only one result — death for the Jews. For hours the attacks went on, while British officials stood by on their balcony and looked on as if they were in a theatre. On successive days, attacks broke out in Hebron, where students and teachers of the Rabbinical school, unarmed and unprotected in their orthodox skull-caps and long coats, were slaughtered like cattle. For in Safed and in other small settlements the government had denied Jews both the right of self-defense and the protection of police and soldiers. The unforeseen savagery of the Arab attack was all the more disastrous because of the equally unforeseen ineptness or even malice of the British government, which punished Jews for carrying arms, their only means of saving their own lives and defending their communities.

It is true, the Arab attacks did not come quite unexpectedly. A whole year of uneasiness and preliminary rumbling had preceded the attacks of 1929. These earlier attacks had centered on the "Wailing Wall," the sole remnant of the ancient Herodian Temple, in Jerusalem. In her "Testimony," Jessie later on pointed out that the British had had ample time to foresee and avoid the violence and the massacres, if they had not followed their ancient policy of "governing by dividing." She was not alone in her impression about the government; Henrietta Szold, speaking before the Hadassah convention later in the same year, could not but accuse the British: "The bitterness of the tragedy flows not from the artificially aroused fanaticism of unlettered assailants. We wondered, almost struck dumb, when our trust in the mature enlightenment of our sponsors was misplaced."

No wonder that Jessie's letters to her sister from August 29 on tell a new and very different story:

> I hope that my cable "SAFE" reached you on time. It is difficult for me to write to you now, because if I write all I want to (write), my letter may not reach you, and there is nothing else for me to write.
>
> Later on, when everything is quiet, I shall probably write you very long letters. Forgive me, if I do not today. I am occupied. . . .

From then on, all of Jessie's letters to America were guarded and cautious; she feared the censor. But she promised to write long letters when everything would once again be quiet. She did more than write letters. She wrote her long passionate "Testimony," which was published in the *New Palestine* (September 29, 1929) and which reads today like an historic document.*

But as was to be expected, she, herself, was deeply dejected, "tired unto death," like the prophet Elijah in the desert. It is significant that she turned to translating Hebrew poetry to keep her mind occupied. Probably some of her magnificent Bialik translations were born in those days of disaster.

Jessie and Tamar spent the days of "trouble" in Tel Aviv, much against Jessie's own judgment. Her friends had persuaded her to stay on in the city, although she felt that "The best place for anyone is Home now." After all, it turned out that she would have been just as safe in Rehoboth. The Arabs knew that there was a strong center of the Haganah (Defense) in Rehoboth, ready to defend the orchards and the fields, so they stayed away from that village.

Jessie — in spite of all her pacifism — was not altogether surprised by these attacks. She had experienced the notorious

---

* See: Appendix B, page 188.

"Easter attack" in her first year in Jerusalem. She even felt: this might happen again. But she had now learned her lesson — and wanted others to learn it too:

> September 12, 1929
>
> . . . It was not a bolt out of the blue, no matter how great a shock it has been. And it may happen again; it may or may not be finished. But with all the agony and resentment, we are only strengthened and more resolutely determined as a result.
>
> We must do all in our power to prevent a repetition, and there are several ways of doing that. These outbreaks are not due to large folk movements but to petty European politics.
>
> Two of the most important means of securing our future are: (1) the unity of the Jews throughout the world in backing us and defending us, and (2) a large and rapid immigration with, of course, the financial backing to make it possible. The way to fight disorder and cowardly crime (and those who foment them) is by increasing the forces of order and raising the international interest in the protection of property and its restitution if destroyed. . . .

One other cruel fact seemed to emerge from the savage attacks:

> September 25, 1929
>
> . . . I hold the British administration here entirely responsible. They had plenty of warning. . . . They wanted and encouraged this outbreak though they did not realize how serious it would be. In general, British policy is to rule by dividing. . . .
>
> This ugly, disgusting, barbarous cruelty is on British hands, though not the hands of the present government in London. What it will or can do remains to be seen. Whatever it does — and so far the trials are ridiculously unfair, Jews put in prison for carrying the arms that alone saved them and their communities, and Arabs put in prison for carrying the arms used in the attack — the Labor Government like all others, will end, and British policy goes on forever.
>
> . . . I am very bitter, very wrathful, very sad and crushed. I see our only hope in these things: a great and rapid strengthening of Jewish capital and immigration (the two must go together in a regular ratio) direct negotiations with the Arab leaders and influencing of intelligent Arab opinion through mutual help and publications (we saw that friendliness with the ignorant Arab peasant does not deter him from violence incited from

above) and the shaping of world opinion in our favor through Jewish steadfast support, moral and financial, in all lands.

If any or all of these fail us, we must still go on. Even a lost cause can have such a power and dignity that it is well lost. But I do believe we shall succeed, though we may have to suffer a great deal to do so. . . .

What Jessie had to say about the results of the Arab attacks on the future of the *Yishuv* and what she recommended in order to forestall future attacks, are as valid today, in 1956, as they were in 1929:

"What is needed now as it was then is: more constructive work by the Jews of the whole world so that all the agony and the resentment of the past will not weaken but strengthen Israel." The poet in Jessie responded differently to those painful impressions. Her "Lamentations" reveal all the distress of the soul whose only weapon is the song:

"In grief there are those who weep
For the tears ooze to ease the pressing glands
And there are those who scream and wring their hands:
And there are those who sleep;
And there are those who when the Scorpions sting,
Can only sing and sing. . . ."

XIV

After the Riots

> Necessity makes murderers of us all,
>   If we would keep on living.
> The gentlest and the sweetest of us all
>   Grow harsh and unforgiving.
> And he whose heart was wise
>   To prune and shape a tree
> Bears in his hands and eyes
>   The lance for injury.
>
> *Hagannah*

The massacres of Hebron and the brutal savagery of the Arab attacks in 1929 seem to mark a basic change in the ideology underlying Jessie's life in Palestine. In her first years in Jerusalem, as we clearly see from her letters, Jessie, like many another tourist in Palestine, seems to have been very much attracted by the Arabs in their Oriental garments. She often mentions her first impression of her Arab "egg-woman — as if she were "risen out of a Doré Biblical portrait." She also maintained a friendly intercourse with her Arab "vegetable man" and felt convinced that the riots which she had witnessed in her first years in Palestine had originated in politics alone. The Arab peasants continued to be fellow-workers and friends of the Jew and had profited by the Jewish immigration; so she argued. They were quite ready to take advantage of the new facilities and to enter Jewish hospitals and maternity wards. Alas! she had to see, in the course of those years, that the friendly peasants and vegetable vendors were

quite as receptive to the inflammatory speeches of the Grand
Mufti as that other, more highly educated people, the Ger-
mans, were to be, when swayed by the speeches of another
Jew-baiter. Still, Jessie's basic view of the great task of Zionism, like the view of Miss Szold, remained steadfast. Both
considered one of the main goals of Zionism to be the establishment of neighborly relations between Arabs and Jews.
Ishmael and his "younger brother," Isaac, as one of her most
appealing poems terms it, would one day in the future live
peacefully side by side, each under his own vine and fig tree.

Did history by-pass Jessie Sampter and Henrietta Szold?
Or is their dream still to be fulfilled, when peace at long last
comes to Israel? Despite contemporary evidence of mutual
hostility between Israel and the Arab states one wonders
whether these two women did not know more about the
gradual development of history than many diehard partisan
politicians.

Of course, some of Jessie's political dreams were strongly
influenced by her friendly relationship with Sir Herbert
Samuel and his earnest and selfless wife, Lady Beatrice, Jessie's
co-worker in communal affairs. For a long time, she felt convinced that this peaceful future would have to be brought
about by the efforts of the British Government. Even in
1927, when she built her house and her sister mentioned the
possibilities of an Arab assault, she answered: "What you say
about Arabs sounds strange to us here. We are safe, in that
respect. In all my years here, I have heard only one case of
a white woman raped by an Arab, and that was in the midst
of the riots of 1920 in Jerusalem. He got several years in
prison."

In 1929, however, this peaceful world and her confidence in
the British were both shattered. But even then she did not
hate the Arabs; they did not know any better and were "out
for loot." But they were savages and had to be educated by

the Yishuv; this remained for her one of the principal aims of Zionism. Now her own bitterness was directed against the British who did not protect the Jews, but, instead, punished them for trying to defend themselves.

It is significant that both Jessie Sampter and Miss Szold at this juncture readily allowed their fellow Jews to hide arms and ammunition in their houses, just as many peace-loving Jews did later on during the War of Liberation. Some years afterwards (1932), we learned from Jessie's letters, she bought herself a strange birthday gift: two guns, and hid them under the tiles of her living room. "May they rest forever!" she prayed. But the fact that she, the lover of peace, deemed this acquisition necessary, reveals more than any lengthy discussion how unsafe her own position and the position of the whole Yishuv seemed to her after the riots of 1929.

This very same feeling kept her from enjoying the peace and privacy of her own new house as deeply as she had enjoyed it in the first years after it was built, when she had felt "ridiculously happy." Perhaps this was one of the reasons which led her after some time to the decision to sell her house and her beloved garden and to give the rest of her private property to the workmen at Givat Brenner.

In 1927, when she won the prize of the Jewish National Fund, she had chosen as her pen-name the name of the woman of Shunem, (*Hashunamit*), who answered the prophet that she did not need anything, as she was "living among her own people." Now the urge to belong to her people, to share with them whatever she had left of her private property grew stronger and stronger. It developed all the more as it grew from her deepest conviction, nourished since her childhood days, that there was something wrong with our economic system. In an article published by the *New Palestine,* August 5, 1927, she revealed her own convictions:

Since I first began to think, I have never been able to take
our economic system for granted. . . . Cash came to me ready
made while others had to work for it. . . . Now I feel that conflict
between employer and employed is unnecessary. . . .

In this same socialist conviction she fully understood the
laborer's rights; and when she built her house, she had made
it a point to say in her contract that "only union and local
labor is to be employed."

Some years earlier, while visiting Emek Jezreel, she had
come across the Collective, the *kevutzah,* or *kibbutz,* which
seemed to her the ideal form of colonization for Palestine.
Here was the social justice of a classless and moneyless society
which she and her American friends had striven to embody
in the ideal of Zionism. After many a discussion with her
faithful and active friend, Leah Berlin, who shared her views
about private property, they came to the conclusion that,
after all, it would be better and more befitting to her life's
socialistic creed, to sell her house and give the money to one
of the new Collective settlements. There, a badly needed
Rest Home "for workmen and teachers" could be established.
This final resolution ripened slowly within the years after
1929. Finally, several reasons impelled her to this act. One
of them was educational: Jessie's main goal in her personal
life was to raise her adopted daughter Tamar in a way that
would best serve Tamar's future. Jessie felt assured that it
was not at all beneficial for Tamar's character to grow up as
"the richest little girl" in the village of Rehoboth. As a member
of the classless society of the Kevutzah Givat Brenner,
Tamar's own social abilities and her sense of social justice
could develop more quickly in the way Jessie wanted to see
them grow.*

---

* Tamar's later life seems to have proved the soundness of Jessie's pedagogical
insight; today, Tamar lives in a *kevutzah,* is married and takes care of her own
children as well as of other people's children.

Another reason for Jessie's final decision to give her private property to the workers and build them a Rest Home was the feeling that thus, at long last, she was fulfilling her own part in the upbuilding of the homeland of Israel. Too frail to work the land and build the roads as the young *Halutzoth* were doing, too weak to guard the settlements as the "Watch-women" did in the times of danger, she wanted the *Bet Hav-raah* (convalescent home) — *Bet Yesha* as it was called after the death of its founder — to represent her own contribution to the upbuilding of the homeland.

However, she was not yet ready, immediately after the riots, for this final decision. Some semi-peaceful years followed the violent emotions of that period. It is true, these years were not without trouble; the fate of the confused world, and the fate of Palestine, most of all, worried Jessie more and more from day to day. Still, there were some happy moments. With her infinite love of life, "which is its own best *raison d'etre,*" she enjoyed them to the full.

Visit To America In 1930

In 1930, Jessie suddenly decided to put into effect a long cherished plan: to visit her sister and, at the same time, to take her daughter, Tamar, to America. As always, her decision came before she could announce her plan to her sister; and once more, Elvie was vacationing and could not be at the station to meet her. This time, the landing was more difficult than the earlier ones, for by now, Jessie had given up her American citizenship and the officials did not allow her and Tamar to land in Boston, which upset her very much. However, her young nephew, Edgar Jr., handled the situation with great competence, signed a guarantee for her, and so brought the painful matter to a happy ending.

It took Jessie some weeks to recover from this initial excitement; but afterwards, the trip proved a success in many respects. Tamar, now a school-girl, attended an American school, and her schoolmates liked her as much as she liked them. Jessie herself took advantage of this American interlude to tell her American friends and the American public something about her life and struggle in Palestine. She gave a series of lectures at Columbia University's International House, which were a great success. Her sister Elvie attended them and was very much impressed, though she was not won over to Zionism. Jessie, in the course of the years, had learned to "husband the amount of strength left to her," as her friend Miss Szold had so often advised her. Now she went to bed as soon as she came home after her lectures and rested. It seemed to her family that this was symbolic of Jessie's whole philosophy of life, ripened with the years. Weak though she might be, she managed to find the strength to do what she earnestly wanted to do, and in this way won all the hard-earned victories of her life.

In April, 1931, Jessie and Tamar sailed back to Palestine and had a delightful trip. Jessie gladly entered into the interests of her young companion; with a sort of vicarious pleasure she described in her letters a costume ball for which she had dressed up Tamar — as an Arab of all things — and made her the Queen of the ball. In fact, Jessie's motherly soul felt very much satisfied by the number of things which Tamar had learned from this trip to the States. It was by traveling that the Sampter girls had learned their geography in their youth; and now Jessie wanted to give Tamar the same pleasurable education, as far as the difficult times allowed. Still, she did not in any way overlook the danger of alienating the young girl from the harsher necessities of the pioneering life in Palestine.

Soon they settled down to their old busy life in Rehoboth. After much soul-searching on Jessie's part and many discussions with her own and Tamar's friends, Tamar was sent to school in Ben Shemen, where she was not only educated in book-lore, but received manual and agricultural training as well, while not neglecting her music.

Jessie's own work with the Yemenites now centered in the kindergarten; it was much more fruitful now that she had acquired the help of that wonderful kindergartner, Maya Rosenberg, whom she had won for her kindergarten in the fateful days of August, 1929, in Tel Aviv. Now Miss Rosenberg was in Rehoboth, and life and work might have been wonderful, had not one dark shadow remained: the financial difficulties, which played a large role in Jessie's reports to her American friends.

Jessie's Friends, Boriz Kazmann and Ben Shlomo

In Rehoboth, Jessie had a close friend and neighbor in Boriz Kazmann, who had been the first to persuade her to come to that village. This man, a tall lean engineer with white hair and vivid deep eyes, was obsessed by an idea to which he sacrificed his whole life without finding due recognition. Jessie had known him long before she came to Palestine; in New York, he had already shown her a sliver of black stone with white veins and told her about the potential fire in the cliffs of the Judaean wilderness. In Rehoboth, Kazmann had established a laboratory in the cellar of his house, where he tried to treat the black limestone from the Dead Sea and develop "oil from the flinty rock." Jessie was vividly interested in his work. She not only took part in his experiments in the cellar, but also recommended him to American friends and notables like Judge Brandeis and Louis Lipsky. But Kazmann died, suddenly, before having completed his great plan.

Life sent Jessie another friend to ease the loneliness of her heart after Kazmann's death. He was a young *halutz* from Austria, who had come to her house in the company of another visitor. She had almost forgotten him, when, after some years,

he came back to see her and they suddenly discovered that
his ideas and aims in life were "exactly like her own," as she
wrote to her sister. "Ben Shlomo" as her letters call him, came
from a family of farmers and rabbis. He had almost completed
his academic studies, when he suddenly decided to abandon
all his plans for a scholarly life and become a farmer in Palestine. Soon he became an expert in orange-culture and found a
job in one of the settlements. After having worked all day,
he would come to Jessie in the evening and they would read
Spinoza together. They also agreed in their ideas about the
Boy Scout work which Jessie had inherited from Dr. Dushkin.
"B.S.," as her letters call him, lived in a hut in Jessie's garden,
and he helped her a great deal with his advice on horticulture
and also on her Boy Scout work.

Jessie openly confessed to her sister that she needed the
friendship of men, "though she could get along without marriage." She felt gratified that her sister understood her uncon-
ventional pattern of friendship and social life in Palestine.

The two friends, Jessie and Ben Shlomo, also shared their
worries. As the young farmer seemed to suffer from some
nervous trouble, Jessie suggested to him her own medicine,
psychoanalysis, which had proved beneficial to her. However,
Jessie was as happy as Ben Shlomo himself when, after some
months in Europe, he came back to her "un-psychoanalyzed,"
while at the same time looking better and feeling better. He
had been able to "help himself," which, after all, was much
to be preferred to any medical treatment. Only now Jessie
confessed in her letters to her sister, how much she missed
him. "It was hard to be without another grown up person,
and a friend" she wrote. Now at long last the two friends were
free to read and discuss. Soon, another link of common interests between them was found; it was the discovery of the
Indian teacher and preacher Krishna Murti, whom Mrs.
Besant had introduced to the world of theosophy and who

seemed to both of them to personify some of the ideas which they themselves had followed all their life. We shall see later on how this common affection for the wisdom of the East brought them together in a joint endeavor to make the wisdom of Krishna Murti available to the world of the Hebrew worker in Palestine.

One last reason may have moved Jessie in her final decision to give up the rest of her private property and also her financial independence for life in a *kevutzah*: this was the financial crisis which in those years came to America as well as to the rest of the world. She often wondered that people in Palestine seemed much less troubled by financial questions than her American friends, though they might have had more cause to worry. Perhaps this also played a part in making her give up her "security," which, at best, was only a false security, and did not protect the American capitalist any better than it did the men in the *kevutzah*.

The center of her communal work remained the care for the Yemenite kindergarten, as her letters to Dr. Dushkin clearly express. Dushkin shared all her satisfaction as well as her worries, in the improvement of Yemenite conditions of life. In March, 1932, she celebrated a grand birthday party with thirty-five Yemenite girls, but her heart was heavy: "we have no money for the Yemenites after Passover. . . ." Luckily, in cases like this, a "miracle" would invariably happen and bring her some money from American friends to carry on her work. In these very same letters to her fellow-worker, she often confessed that, without this help from across the sea, she could not have kept up her work, as both the Zionist institutions and Hadassah itself had too many obligations to support this important activity as well.

And so Jessie Sampter, in these years, was wavering between satisfaction and depression; but her satisfaction won out. At odd intervals, she enjoyed working on the third edition of her

Guide to Zionism. Though she had at first tried to get rid of this labor of love, being convinced that the work could be done better and more quickly in America, she could not now help enjoying both the thought that it was needed and the work of preparing it. As we already mentioned, she had chosen a novel form for her *Modern Palestine*, a forum, which made it possible for a number of prominent Jews to inform the reader about the achievements in Palestine. Of course, it meant a great deal of letter writing for her as the editor, but she had the satisfaction of knowing that the book was favorably received by the entire American press.

With this satisfying survey of past and present achievements in Palestine, the year 1933 seemed to begin auspiciously for Jessie Sampter and for the Jews of the world. Nobody knew that it was destined to be a year of disaster and unforeseen savagery of attack, one of the darkest years in all Jewish history, but at the same time a year of refuge for the terror-stricken Jews of Germany. Here, too, God had created the remedy before the sickness, the refuge before the persecution. And the name of the remedy was: Palestine.

XV

From Rehoboth to the Kibbutz

> I have at the last moment made a very
> radical change in my plans. . . . I decided
> to do this: To build the house in the Kib-
> butz called Givat Brenner . . .; to sell my
> house; to turn the capital I have here in to
> the *kibbutz* and become a member. . . .
> The conditions I am making are: that the
> Rest Home be vegetarian and that I have a
> suitable room in it, and my living in it,
> for the rest of my life. When I built my
> house, I knew it to be impermanent, a
> transition. This next step is as permanent
> as my coming to Palestine and perhaps no
> less radical.
> I realize that.
> From Jessie's Letter to her sister,
> June 19, 1933.

In order to understand fully what impelled Jessie
Sampter, in the years after the riots of 1929, to become a member of the *kevutzah* Givat Brenner and to give up her own
dearly loved home in Rehoboth, we shall have to look at the
political situation of the Yishuv in those years. The violent
outburst of the Arabs in 1929 was succeeded by an unforeseen
political windfall which tended to persuade the Arabs that
"violence worked." The British sent Lord Passfield to investi-
gate. After many deliberations and futile efforts, the result
was the notorious White Paper, which nullified the Balfour

Declaration and the Mandate, absolved the Grand Mufti and
the administration, and severely curtailed Jewish immigration.
A storm of protests from both Jewish and Gentile authorities
set in; and, in response, a letter written by Ramsay MacDon-
ald to Dr. Weizmann admitted the British obligation towards
the Jewish people, but tried to restrict Jewish immigration in
accordance with the "economic capacity" of Palestine. The
Arabs, therefore, had ample reason to rejoice, while the Jews
were sorely disappointed.

Jessie felt keenly that these political difficulties might en-
danger the future of Jewish Palestine, although in her stub-
born optimism she did not consider the situation hopeless.
Still another difficulty made her uneasy: the American economic collapse in 1929 deprived the Zionist movement of its
most prominent and most generous contributors. We have
already mentioned that Jessie had to conclude her gay report
on her "birthday party with 35 Yemenite girls" in 1932 with
the wistful sentence: "My heart is heavy . . . we shall not have
any money after Passover." For the same reason, her letters
to her sister abound in open or implied requests for "un-
labeled money" instead of a birthday present. She always was
in need of some extra cash for her Yemenite work, or some
individual cases of distress.

As to her own financial situation, she had after many deliberations and negotiations with her American "minister of
finance," her brother-in-law, Edgar Wachenheim, decided
against buying an orange grove, much as she wanted to do so
in order to help a friend to get a job in it. Now she planned
to use the rest of her funds in America to publish her poems
and so realize a long cherished wish. However, in January,
1932, she startled her family by cabling: "Don't publish
poems!" She had decided, after all, that there were more "living, vital things" for her to do with her money, which she
could not do after her death. It is true, she said, her poems

were living too; but they had attained independence and were living a timeless life. They might be published after her death, like Emily Dickinson's poems. In her next letter, so she promised, she would tell them what the "living vital things" were for which she wanted to use her funds. For the time being, she only hinted that they were connected with her friend, Leah Berlin, and their plans to live out their lives together. However, Jessie stressed the fact that the decision itself was her own and not Leah Berlin's.

In a later letter, Jessie comes back to her mysterious decision and her refusal to publish her own poems: "This book will be published some day, and why hurry. . . ."

It is a gratifying thought that, in effect, her poems, the harvest of a lifetime, as she liked to call them, were after all published in her lifetime and favorably received by the Jewish and Gentile press all over the world. This is the often quoted volume, *Brand Plucked from the Fire,* published by the Jewish Publication Society of America in 1937.

THE EFFECT OF THE GERMAN HOLOCAUST

The next year, 1933, brought another catastrophe for the Jews in Europe. It taught Jessie that there are more living and vital things to consider than just "publicity." Again, as in 1929, Jessie's reports in her letters were cautious and guarded because of her constant fear of the censor. But her poems, and now and then an unguarded line in her letters too, betray how deeply the disaster of the German Jews shocked her. These eloquent poems are not included in the collection of poems which came out in 1937, but were published in American Jewish magazines as they were written. The "Sonata Passionata" tried to decipher the enigma of the German mind which can be a God and a beast, a Beethoven and a Hitler. From the poet's helpless misery and startled amazement there at last emerges a feeling of blessed relief: "Thank God that

there is a haven for Jewish youth in Palestine!" The same
feelings of distress, in those years, brought Jessie's friend,
Henrietta Szold, to the realization of the brilliant idea of the
German Jewess, Recha Freyer — the creation of the modern
Children's Crusade, the "Youth Aliyah," which saved the lives
of many thousands of Jewish children.

This, too, was the feeling that finally moved Jessie Sampter
to give up the rest of her private property in order to create
something which would benefit all suffering Jews. At first, she
planned to buy a small piece of land and establish a rest
home on a small experimental scale. "It is an educational
matter; and it is of a piece with the whole life around us."
Gradually, her plan developed and became clearer in her own
mind. To make it more palatable to her "financial advisors"
in America, she shrewdly stressed the fact that it might be an
excellent investment. The heart of the matter is: she planned
to establish a rest home which was badly needed and to
charge only the prices which workmen and simple people
could afford.

The Rest Home At Givath Brenner

The American bank crisis had demonstrated to her that
there was no security in money-matters anywhere in the world.
"American tourists run around like chickens without
heads . . ." she wrote in March 1933; and she had to
smile a little at the consternation of the very people whom
she had unmercifully portrayed in her *Emek* as begoggled,
becameraed and turning up their noses at the Jewish workers. . . ."

Of course, she was willing to submit obediently to the decision of her "finance minister" and her sister, should they
decide against it. She expected a cable, "Delay!" But their
understanding hearts knew how to answer; they sent her the
rest of her capital and acceded to her plan, possibly not without some qualms.

Bet Yesha, the Rest House at Givat Brenner

From then on her personal feelings and worries played a minor role in her letters. The main theme was her burning interest in her "creation," the Rest Home. Gradually, this new plan developed and the site of the Rest Home was changed. At first, she had planned to build it on the highest spot available, in a pine grove. In June 1933, as a result of consultations, her final plans ripened and assumed a somewhat new aspect. She and Leah Berlin decided to join the *kevutzah* as members. On June 19, 1933, she wrote, with some solemnity, well knowing that this would be a startling decision for her relatives:

> I have at the last moment made a very radical change in my plans. . . . We were about to build, all the plans were ready. . . . Then I had a talk with Leah which set me thinking a great deal. After it, I decided to do this:
> (1) To build the house in the *kibbutz* called Givat Brenner, which is about 2 miles south of Rehoboth on a high and very beautiful hill.
> (2) To sell my house and
> (3) To turn the capital I have here in to the *kibbutz* and become a member. . . .
> One of my chief reasons is: that I want to escape from the necessity of balancing my budget. . . .
> The condition: that the Rest Home be vegetarian and that I have a suitable room in it for the rest of my life. . . .
> When I built this house, I knew it to be impermanent . . . a transition. . . . This next step is as permanent as my coming to Palestine and perhaps no less radical.
> I realize that.

Of course, her anxious sister could not help sending her a troubled letter full of questions. Jessie understood her agitation, but reminded her:

> July 6, 1933
> . . . Remember that you've always feared or disapproved my decisions and usually agreed with them after the event. I hope the same will prove true this time.
> This — like others — is a decision that has been long growing. Even when I built my house, I went first through the Emek and tried to find a way of hitching my life with a *kevutzah* or *moshav*. None near Rehoboth, and I wanted to be here, from personal,

social and climatic reasons. So I built my house. I did so with an
inner reservation to keep myself free of it, that is: to sell it whenever I wanted to go elsewhere. I did not think it would be permanent. . . .

The economic strain of living in this house and garden is too
great. I want to be free of the continual figuring to make both
ends meet. . . .

I have not yet an offer for my house, but with the large middle-
class immigration I think I should be able to sell it well. . . .
I am in no hurry.

The only question which seemed to worry Jessie a little in
this tremendous new decision was: Did she do Tamar a wrong
in depriving her of her heritage? Jessie seems to have pon-
dered this question for a long time; then she came to the
conclusion:

. . . In the long view, I believe I am doing what she (Tamar)
would have me do. I can only hope so. There is a strong possibility that a high school for the workers' children is to be started
at *Kevutzah Shiller*, 10 minutes from Brenner. In that case she
(Tamar) can be with me!

One reason for being loathe to leave her house and garden
was mentioned and rejected. It was hard to leave the garden
and the trees which she herself had planted.

But six years ago, this was bare earth; and in 3 years I can have
as lovely a garden again on what is now bare earth. That is the
joy of creation!

Elvie's fifth and last question, whether Jessie would find in
Givat Brenner the privacy which she needed for her poetical
work, was also answered:

I will probably have more seclusion and privacy than now. Going
back to country life, I expect to have my own room, fairly
large, with 2 couches, and my own wash-stand, and a screened
porch before it. I shall probably be alone most of the day. But
groups of young people (will come to me) practically every
evening. That is what I want.

There remains one reason which Jessie held in the background for fear that it would not mean so much to her American relatives as it meant to her: that was the German tragedy. She felt: in America, they read about it in newspapers, always with the suspicion that these might be "horror stories" and that not all of them were true, and what they wished to believe, they readily believed. But here in Palestine, you know the tragedy of the German Jews. And now, in spite of all her fear of the censor, her agony came out into the open:

> They have been root and branch Germans for generations. This should lead to a deep breakup of the illusion of separate nationalism. I am glad they are coming here, to shield us against the poison of exaggerated Jewish nationalism. All the horrors of the world will leave something true and real after the cleansing process. . . .

It was this "unparalleled tragedy of the German Jews" which quickened her resolution to build the Rest Home.

> It makes Palestine even more vital as a haven for these refugees who are passionately fond of German culture. Already German children are sent to Palestine and saved from humiliation and death. In Rehoboth, there is no family without its German refugees.
> In fact: it is the only way to bear these awful times, if you are able to do something to help.

Thereafter, Jessie Sampter again and again returned in her letters to this twofold feeling — her agony about the tragedy of the German Jews, and the feeling of blessed relief that there was a Palestine to be a haven for the persecuted Jews. All this added to her own deep satisfaction of living in a *kibbutz,* in a community of mutually responsible individuals.

> . . . All economic worries are taken from me, also all household worries. I cannot imagine better security in this uncertain world. I become a member of a community who consider themselves responsible for my welfare as I for theirs. *I have been very happy at times in my life (all suffering seems as nothing to me now). But I think I have never been quite as happy as I am now. And I*

have no fear of life. . . . I don't feel that my money is mine; that
is the strange attitude I have to possession. I have to share it. . . .

This deeply felt harmony and satisfaction constantly appear
in Jessie's letters from the time she decided to become a member of the *kibbutz* Givat Brenner. She was living where she
wanted to live — in a country which she had helped to build
up; and — what was even more satisfying — in the midst of a
community which represented the ideal she had dreamed
about ever since she grew up, that of a classless and moneyless
society.

The basic harmony of Jessie Sampter's being remained constant in all the trouble and pain with which the "confused
state of the world" burdened her last years. There might have
been a halo around the frail woman who, in all the terror and
desperation of those days remained optimistic, happy and
always occupied with some creative work.

XVI

Life in a Kibbutz

> . . . I have been very happy at times in
> my life, (all the suffering seems as nothing
> to me now) ; but I think I have never been
> quite so happy as I am now. And I have
> no fear of life. . . . I don't feel that my
> money is mine; that is the strange attitude
> I have to possession. I have to share it. . . .
>
> From Jessie's Letter to her sister, July 7, 1933

From then on, Jessie Sampter's life in the *kibbutz* (or: *kevutzah,* as she sometimes calls this community)
seemed to run on an even keel. Of course, there were minor
irritations, as the building of the Rest Home was delayed;
there were, as everywhere, human frailties and errors of
administration, which Jessie neither overlooked nor hid from
her correspondents. And there was the gloomy background of
this gay and buoyant picture — the tragedy of the German
Jews and the general uncertainty of the world which extended
to Palestine, too. But at that time Jessie seemed so even-tem-
pered that even in this heartbreaking calamity she found some
encouragement. As she and Miss Szold well knew, the only
way of holding out in those tragic times was by helping somebody else. And that is what they were able to do in Palestine
by sheltering many unhappy children and raising them in a
free country to a life of freedom and work. So Jessie tried to
smile away her depression by telling her sister about the dif-

ferent interpretations of the marriage laws which were per-
missible in those times of stress. After mentioning to her how
a friend of hers had married a German refugee girl in order
to shield her from deportation, she confessed that she herself
would not mind marrying a refugee if she could thereby "save
him from that awful fate," even if it would mean her having
to practice "polyandry," by marrying two men at one and the
same time. "Did you know that you had such a wicked sister?"
she gaily wound up her weekly report.

Evidently, at that time of her life, when all the world trem-
bled and she, of all people, sensed danger and tragedy drawing
near, Jessie had the feeling that she had gone the right way
to her goal; her love of life had deepened and she felt the joy
of living — living pure and simple — more intensely than ever
before.

Her relatives in America, on their part, were a little uneasy
about Jessie's revolutionary step in selling her house — though
they were glad to hear that she got a good price for it — and
giving the rest of her private property to the new community.
It is easily understandable that Jessie had first of all to try to
ease their worries about her own future. In the beginning,
she had planned to keep a typewritten diary in order to have
her sister and her American friends share with her the life of
this new and astonishing cooperative community. But soon
after she came to Givat Brenner she found out that there was
too much to do for her to concentrate on keeping such a diary.
So she tried to describe, in her letters to her anxious relatives
and friends, the essence of this new experiment in living. First
she explained the fundamentals of the *kibbutz,* and afterwards
she described her own day in Givat Brenner. Here is what she
wrote about the basic ideas of the *kibbutz:*

February 12, 1934
This is a commune of 280 grown people and 280 children
between the ages of one week and 8 years . . . then there is a

jump to the age of 18, with only 2 or 3 little German visitors in between, who attend school in the village. The older people range up to 60 or 70 years, these being parents of members and some of them also members of the *kibbutz*.

. . . Everyone works here. One could not live here and not work; it would be a spiritual impossibility. One long-bearded father is doing accounts, older women work in the Store House mending or darning. Now, in a good season, about 100 members work in the village at farm work or other vocations. Some are in the cooperative bakery which supplies the village. We have a carpenter shop, including fine cabinet making, and a cafeteria in the village, both doing very well. Here we have a foundry which makes our own beds and also takes outside orders. We are economically independent in large measure, as we have almost every trade and profession in our membership. We have an excellent electrician . . . a dentist who receives patients from all the neighboring *kevutzot*, builders, brick makers — all the work on the Rest Home is being done by our own members — and, of course, dress-makers, tailors, shoe-makers, mattress makers, plumbers, and so on. We grow most of our own produce — all that is grown in Palestine, I think — and we sell citrus fruit, dairy products, eggs, vegetables, saplings and flowers. Every Friday our girls have a flower-market in Rehoboth. And, incidentally, every member can have flowers or a little plant on his table. We have a very fine incubator and sell eggs and chickens for breeding purposes. . . .

Now to the social side: We are frightfully short of buildings and overcrowded. We want to take in as many people as possible — as the economic situation allows — and especially the German youth. The result is gravely inadequate sleeping and living quarters. We are just going through a very bad rain and wind storm, and it is no joke for those who live three and four in a tent. . . .

The children are well-housed but also overcrowded. The old people and the weaker members are in the best houses. And new houses are built rapidly. There are several going up now. We foresee the economic possibility of increasing the group to 500, and must plan accordingly. . . .

The children eat in their own house. We now have a very good dining-hall — lately renewed and so pleasant that it has practically become a living-room as well — and a new kitchen which is a model one. It was very bad, and now it is very good. It would do credit to a good hotel, with all modern labor-saving devices. . . . We need a reading room and a culture hall. Our

Library is inadequately housed, very large, catalogued for distribution, but with no place to sit and read. We are planning a good room and have already some of the money for it.

My own room — as I wrote you — is very good, even in a storm, and I am now sharing it with Leah, because I cannot demand a room for myself under present conditions. In the Rest Home I shall have my own room. . . .

The membership is very varied in nationality, culture and education. . . . No one is supposed to have any money, and the question of gift moneys is one that occupies our minds at times. The real problem of course is not that of money but of prejudices . . . mental limitations of all kind. . . . I find most of those members whom I know satisfied that this is the type of life they want. There is a great deal of suffering; there is very much happiness. My gravest criticism is: too much work and too little privacy for most of its members. . . .

Later on, Jessie had to reply to some of her correspondent's objections:

Yes, all work for the community is done without remuneration. All pay to individual workers goes into the common fund. Leah just got a pair of sandals, which cost her a walk to our shoemaker's, behind the dining-hall. The dentist has a very well-equipped office two rooms away from me, and I was there this morning to have a sensitive spot treated. Anything I need from Tel Aviv — need, not want — is ordered for me by our storekeeper. Things also are paid if they are necessary, or if there are funds enough to indulge in vacations or outings — according to need and turn, and I am sure that any trip I wanted to take to visit Tamar would be paid without questions.

Life here is very free, and there is a great deal of personal consideration. Each one is treated according to his needs. . . . The ideal which guides us is, as far as possible, to give to each his needs, and get from each whatever he can give.

As you say, it does not always work out so well. Still, I should decidedly call this experiment a great success, not in relation to the ideal, but in comparison with life in other places.

We see from this letter that Jessie Sampter, the girl from the spacious "Sampter Mansion" on Fifth Avenue, seems to have adjusted very easily to the primitive living conditions of the *kibbutz* and to her own plain room "No 7" which, as her friends felt, "seemed to reach out into the world." No wonder that she felt at home! This sort of society seemed to her to be the fulfillment of a dream which she had harbored ever since she first felt "that there was something wrong about cash that came to her ready-made without her having worked for it." Here, as she told her sister, she was "feeling well and working hard," both with her writing and her "handwork of love." Her skillful fingers helped to decorate the dining-room tables, knitted a bright red sweater for a little girl of seven, cut silhouettes for the Children's House. Between times, she managed to write English and Hebrew poems, which came to her while resting, for she had always felt convinced that "poetry comes while you sleep."

"We are as happy as this crazy world and the newspapers allow us to be"— this is the ever-recurring refrain of her letters. Here is a typical day in her life in those first years in the *kibbutz*.

> . . . Life here goes on as naturally as if I had never lived any other. . . . I have undertaken many activities — perhaps too many — but things will adjust themselves according to the possibilities. I'll give you a description of my day; so perhaps gradually you will get a conception of what life is like here. Leah and I sleep in one room for the present. We each have an electric bed lamp. Generally we both wake at about six. I light mine and knit or crochet for an hour. I don't like to read then. Leah gets up at 6:45, she starts her work in the kitchen at 7. At 7, a young girl — who worked for us before we came here — comes in, lights my oil stove and brings me hot water for washing. At 8 she brings me breakfast and cleans the room, etc. At 9, I begin to write and have the whole morning for my work, in bad weather in the room, in fine weather on the porch. At 12:45 I either go to lunch in the dining room or have it brought to my room, according to weather and health. I sleep ½ hour till 2. From 2 to 3 I study alone. I am now reading Job with commentary. At 3 some girls come to me for an hour's study of Hebrew — newcomers — we are reading Genesis.
>
> From 3-6 I do various sorts of handwork, now chiefly in connection with decorating the new children's houses, making dolls,

etc. I have guests, too, sometimes. In the evenings, twice a week
I have an advanced English group reading Shelley's poetry.
Sometimes there are meetings.

Saturday is the one day spent almost entirely with people,
groups, etc. This week my Yemenite youth came up.

The fearful happenings in Austria made us search our hearts.
I cannot comfort myself with slogans and the "International,"
so I have to do a lot of thinking — some of it aloud. . . .

KRISHNA MURTI

What did she think about in these first years in Givat Brenner? Her letters tell us something more about the main contents of her thoughts. In those days of seeming peace amidst a
world of war and turmoil, her thoughts returned again and
again to the Indian teacher and preacher, Krishna Murti, in
whom she had been very much interested for some years past.
Her friend, Ben Shlomo, had attended the Ommen Camp in
Holland, where Krishna Murti gave a series of lectures. He
came back full of enthusiasm and had told her more about
this man, whose ideas about communal living seemed to be
very similar to their own ideas in the *kibbutz*. Now the two
of them, Ben Shlomo and Jessie, decided to make Krishna
Murti's teaching available to the whole community of workers in Palestine, who seemed predestined to understand this
man and to learn from him. With Jessie's "precious birthday
money" sent by her sister, she planned to publish a booklet
of selected essays by Krishna Murti, translated into Hebrew.
She herself arranged the material and wrote the English Introduction. They called this booklet *Al Ha-Ikar* (About the
Fundamentals). and it was printed by the Kibbutz Ha-meuhad
(United Settlements) in Ein Harod.

In her Introduction, Jessie informs her readers about the
life and the basic ideas of Krishna Murti. He was a youth
from India who was discovered by Annie Besant, the leader
of the theosophists, and carefully educated in England. It
seems that Miss Besant saw in him a future "Teacher of the

World," a Messiah. However, the young Brahmin himself renounced this world-leadership, and in 1929, he dissolved the "Order of the Eastern Star," which Miss Besant had founded to propagate the new religion. This — so it seems — is what endeared him most of all to Jessie Sampter. She stressed, in the Introduction, that Krishna Murti did *not* want to become a world-teacher; everybody would have to find his own way. Religion is a matter for the individual and has to be discovered by Everyman, by an inner enlightenment. One thing and one only did Krishna Murti wish his disciples to learn: to think.

This was what Jessie, herself, had always proclaimed as the aim and only goal of her own educational efforts. Like Krishna Murti, she had always felt that the gist of any religion lies in doing, not in believing; that is what the *kibbutz* had taught her again after she had realized it through her own whole life.

One more lesson of Krishna Murti's appealed to her most strongly. He had written a book, *The Kingdom of Happiness,* in which he had taught his disciples to enjoy life with all their might, both with their rational and their emotional powers. It is touching to see how Jessie Sampter, this much-suffering woman, tried to adopt this optimistic maxim and to lift her head above the dark waters of despair, which she knew only too well. Krishna Murti taught her own dearly-bought wisdom: life is good in its laughter and in its tears. Here was the love of life in its entirety, which she had so often proclaimed as the beginning and the end of her wisdom. She may have felt reminded by these ideas of Krishna Murti's of her earliest days, of her adored father and of his "abundant love of life."

We can readily understand why she wrote: "This book deals with just that inner side of social living, the motivation, which is needed in order to make such a group as ours a success. . . . It deals with that inner revolution without which all outer

forms of change are merely a shell which again comes to serve
the oppressors and the exploiters. . . ."

The Construction Of The Rest Home

As is usual in such undertakings, the construction of the
"Rest Home" lagged behind schedule, and Jessie had to wait
a long time until her room in the *Beth Havraah* was ready to
receive her. In the meantime, she had suffered several attacks
of bronchitis and felt that she needed a house of her own and
somebody to take care of her physical wants. After much
deliberation, she found a solution to this problem in her own
individual way. She went to stay with a young Yemenite
woman, Kadia, whom she had known for a long time and who
had worked for her before. Kadia was a splendid housewife
and happy to help her adored friend and teacher; she did
everything "with a happy face." Moreover, she was the inspiration of one of Jessie's most significant poems, "Kadia," which
was published by *Opinion* and illustrated by Ruth Light-
Kazman (*Opinion*, May, 1935). In this work, the young Yemenite mother talks to her baby and rejoices that her little daughter will no more know "child marriage and slave life," as her
grandmother and mother had known them. All of Jessie's
own work for the Yemenite women forms the background of
this poetical gem.

In 1934, though the Rest Home was not quite ready, Jessie
for the first time in her life enjoyed a real *Kibbutz* Seder in
her own surroundings. The first evening of the Passover Festival was "totally untraditional in its form and totally traditional in its spirit," as she wrote to her sister. The children
acted out the crossing of the Red Sea and wound up the evening by singing and dancing. The whole festival was transformed into a children's festival, and so may, in a way,
have realized its original scriptural meaning: "Thou shalt tell
it to thy son." Such a coming-alive of one of the three Biblical

harvest festivals brought deep moral satisfaction to Jessie, who had longed for a religious revival ever since she came to Palestine. Of course, she did not overlook the fact that the "Solemn Festivals," the Days of Awe (Yamin Noraim) did not yet partake in this revival. "There is an empty space between Rosh Hashanah and Sukkoth" she wrote a little later in her "Confession." . . . But the three festivals — Passover, Pentecost, Sukkoth — showed a new face. They made her hope that the messianic revival, the bringing near of the hearts of the parents to the hearts of the children, as the prophet termed it, (Malachi 3:24) was yet to come. She never lost this hope.

JESSIE'S OWN WRITING IN GIVAT BRENNER.

Ever so gradually, Jessie Sampter's own literary efforts entered a new phase. It is a rare thing for a poet to acquire in his maturity a new language as medium of his poetry; but that is what Jessie Sampter did. From her first day in Palestine she had both taught English and learned Hebrew. But only now, in April, 1934, did she feel ready to write her first Hebrew story "about a little Yemenite girl." It was published in *Davar*, the Labor daily.*

*In spite of all my investigations in America and Israel (at the Zionist Archives, the Hebrew Union College and the *Davar* in Jerusalem) I have not been able to find any copies of Jessie Sampter's contributions to *Davar*, so that her Hebrew poetry can be treated here only very cursorily. We have to be satisfied with reading her numerous contributions in English magazines like the *Jewish Frontier* and *Opinion*, which very significantly portray the life at Givat Brenner and the problems of the day.

Opinion (1932-38) published her poems "Silence" (December, 1932) and the "Palestinian Poems" (1935) which were vividly illustrated by Ruth Light-Kazman. Also some prose selections "Comment on Anti-Semitism" which won a prize, and the already quoted poem, "Beethoven's Sonata Passionata," her pained study of the German mind. One of her finest and most significant poems is "Testament to Esther the Gardener" (September, 1937. All these poems which are hard to obtain nowadays would bear a new edition as they reveal a new phase of Jessie Sampter's poetry.

The *Jewish Frontier* published: "The Badge," (Jan. 1936) (a snapshot from the Life in the Kibbutz); "A Quiet Morning Hour," (Aug. 1936); "In Memoriam to a Working Girl," (A Yemenite story) (Aug. 1936); "Watchwomen," (biographical sketches of several Palestine pioneer women) (Nov. 1936).

Some time in those years, the great poet Bialik died in Tel
Aviv, "the greatest Hebrew poet of our days or perhaps since
the golden period of Spanish culture" as Jessie termed it. She
felt moved by this news to define her own general position on
poetry and to comment on the difference, in responsiveness
to poetry, between readers in America and Hebrew readers
in Palestine:

> Givat Brenner, July 9, 1934
> When Bialik died, the whole country went into mourning,
> and all festivities were postponed. Every Hebrew paper was dedi-
> cated to him and carried reprints of his poems. I suspect that
> even you will read of it and notice it in the N. Y. *Times,* some-
> thing which I think would hardly happen in the case of any
> living poet in America.
> I write all this only to call attention to the anachronism of a
> people interested in poets and poetry. Bialik is the highlight,
> but poets and poetry in general are beloved . . . and the memory
> of certain poets is deeply cherished, such as the woman worker
> Rahel, who was a friend of mine and who died of TB three
> years ago, while I was on the journey back from America.
> Her (Rahel's) poems are not only read but sung.
> Curiously, it was just about that time, while I was on the
> steamer and did not yet know of her death, that I began to
> occupy myself seriously with the writing of Hebrew poetry. I
> served a long apprenticeship, and it is less than a year ago that
> I offered for publication and had published two short poems in
> the supplement of the Labor Daily, Davar. Since then I had a
> story of Yemenite life published, and now I have several more
> things about to appear, among them five poems. The day after
> Bialik died, I made a little poem about him . . . which I read at
> our memorial meeting in the evening and which will now be
> published.
> Why am I writing this long story? You will guess right that
> it is to point a moral, and a very personal one. Years ago, when I
> joined the Poetry Society, where all the poets went to pat each
> other on the back, I soon discovered that in America poetry is
> appreciated almost alone by poets, and that the few others who
> love it are near-poets or feel lonely and peculiar. I discovered
> something else when I began to write for Zionists. For the first
> time, I felt that unique response of love which is the poet's
> reward as it is the lover's reward . . . for which he did not ask.

But it is a fact that with the popularization of Zionism in America this warm folk feeling disappeared, that today, poetry is no longer published in Zionist papers, or, when it does appear, has taken on exactly the same character of a subordinate intellectual game as in other papers. Only here did I discover how beautiful and joyous can be the response of lovers of poetry to the poet whom they love.

I believe I understand the reasons. I also believe that "anachronism" may refer to the future as well as to the past. I believe poetry will be loved in America with a love that has perhaps never been known there before. I cannot guess what kind of poetry it will be, but it will surely be "simple, sensuous and passionate."

I would continue to write poetry, perhaps in both languages, even if it were not published. Creation is growth, not plan, and so the first part does not depend on the next. But publication is as truly a part of the creative process in writing as birth is as creative as conception. Publication played no part as the purpose of a writing. Yet that which is written is for publication . . . finally. It seems to me that there is nothing in the world which I especially want except the publication of the collection of my poems — *now*. Something inexplicable — to myself — urges me now to do this. I have tried in vain to analyze it; I cannot, but I trust it. And somehow I expect my friends to understand. I have to ask some cooperation from them . . . which means trouble . . . because I cannot possibly do it from here. But my feeling is . . . maybe I am mistaken? . . . that they will be compensated by the book itself.

"It certainly seems as if no one here is interested enough to do anything. . . ." That quotation from your letter, Sister dear, is what has called forth most of this letter.

World Situation In 1933-1938

Ever since 1933, the successes of Hitler and Mussolini had encouraged the Arabs in Palestine to follow in their footsteps. Eventually, Arab terror spread all over the country and every night the *Shmirah* (Guard) had to protect the crops and settlements as well as their own lives. We do not find much about this in Jessie's letters, as she was again afraid that the censor would not allow such information to get by, and that, in such a case, her beloved sister would remain without mail. But the

constant tension is implicit in all her letters and grows more
intense with every day. Three elements predominate in her
weekly reports: her busy, creative and deeply satisfied life in
the *kibbutz*, her wish to see her poems eventually published
in America, "the safest and sanest of countries," and her intense
fear that the future would entangle all of the world in war.
Sometimes it would seem as if this shy and peace-loving
woman was indeed something of a prophet; she seems to have
foreseen the Second World War, which she did not live to
witness.

In those years, the Jews in Palestine were having their own
serious troubles. In 1933, the Zionist Congress had voted a
solemn protest against the terror in Germany and had called
upon the Mandatory Power, which had guaranteed the Balfour Declaration in 1920, to open the doors of Palestine for
as large a German immigration as possible. It was the first of a
series of appeals which fell on deaf ears. But in spite of British
reluctance, in the years 1933-35, some 50,000 German immigrants had come to Palestine. They not only brought new skills
and industries to the land, but also, by means of the ingenious
institution of the *Haavarah*, were allowed to save part of their
money and bring it to Palestine. In this way Palestine was
able to absorb a larger number of the German exiles than any
other country in the world. In consequence, there was building and orange growing in Palestine while there was depression in America. However, while the German exiles were
happy to have found a home and at the same time helped to
build up the country, the Arabs launched a full-scale revolt
against the Balfour Declaration; and they were encouraged
by the half-hearted, ambiguous policy of the British. In fact,
they hoped that the Balfour Declaration might be repudiated.
Armed Arab bands roamed the countryside; they uprooted
the trees, killed the farmers and burnt the crops. A new problem arose for the Jews: should they retaliate "in kind?" Were

they justified in meeting violence with violence? Jewish extremists answered "yes."

Jessie Sampter had been a pacifist all her life (except for a short while when she and some "millions of other dupes," to quote herself, had been deluded by President Wilson's message about the "war to end all wars"). It follows naturally that she now felt depressed by this extremist reaction. "It is the greatest danger," she wrote, "that the Jews will not continue their discipline of non-reprisal . . ." (March 15, 1937).

In 1937, American Zionists had voted against the partition of Palestine. They favored a bi-national state. Jessie, as we saw, fully agreed to this ideal. She had given her own answer long ago in her poem, "Ishmael, my Brother." Now she had to see what she considered the darkest tragedy of all the tragedies of her life: "What is worse: some of our young Jewish Fascists are responsible for the bombs thrown at Arabs in Jerusalem! This is the greatest calamity that could befall us!" Of course, even she was not all starry-eyed and willing to let her people be victimized without fighting back. She learned about the necessity for the Hagannah, which had protected her own Rehoboth in the dark days of 1929, but she could not close her eyes to the fact that "Necessity makes murderers of us all."

> "And he whose heart was wise
> To prune and shape a tree
> Bears in his hands and eyes
> The lance for injury. . . ."
> *Hagannah*

Gradually these two contrasting elements seemed to shape life in Givat Brenner (as in all Palestine):

> It is a garden of Eden . . . inside a ring of fire that comes closer and closer . . . (July 26, 1938).

Still, she continued to derive from her own peaceful surroundings the inner strength to keep on hoping:

> July 18, 1938
> Over us hangs the smoke and cloud of the European holocaust. . . . As for us — I cannot be a pessimist. There is so much that is true, good, healthy, in human life that it will find the true way to build after the old rotten house burnt down.
> I am sitting under my tree — it is beautiful. The breeze is sweet. And the world is on fire!

Here are some more pictures from those years in order to illustrate more clearly the fateful contrasts of her peaceful life in a world of war:

> July 4, 1938: Independence Day
> Dear Sister:
> Here, it is peaceful, though the world is full of war, even right around me. I found a wonderful little "work-room" under an eucalyptus tree at the end of our garden, tall and leafy, in a grove of cedars, a miniature forest. There I put my deck chair and hide every forenoon. . . . I long to be with you. . . . I enclose a leaf of the eucalyptus tree. If you break it, you will get the eucalyptus smell. Our house is crowded, people I know and like: one of my "boys" from Rehoboth, now a young father, a clerk in the village council. . . .
> Givat Brenner has a summer camp this year. 25 children from 6-12 years. All seem to be satisfied with the camp. . . . But there is a tragedy at Ramat Hakovesh: a bomb killed eight members of the community. . . .

> July 26, 1938
> It is so beautifully cool where I am sitting now under this drooping eucalyptus tree with young cedars around me and a tiny bird slipping in and out of his nest — that it is just hard to remember that outside it is unendurably hot and that in the country all around us murder and destruction are running wild. . . .
> I would not leave now, even if I could. I send you some Honesty* grown from your seeds.

---

* Mrs. Wachenheim used to send her flower seeds, which she planted in the garden at Givat Brenner.

So life went on peacefully in Givat Brenner, while in Jerusalem and all over the country terror reigned. This fearful situation was brought very near to Jessie by a young American journalist who came to Givat Brenner, and to whom we owe the most vivid accounts of Jessie Sampter's last years —Dorothy (Ruth) Kahn. This gifted young writer who had read some of Jessie's books, had become so enthusiastic that she had to be near her heroine, and did not hesitate to make her home in a *"liftvan"* (wardrobe case) brought by the German immigrants, since the Rest Home was crowded at the moment. Dorothy Kahn's articles give us an eyewitness' impression of the way in which Jessie Sampter's last years were spent. As we see her every-day life in Givat Brenner best in Dorothy Kahn's essays, it seemed to me that I could do no better than let this eye witness speak. Here is Miss Kahn's description of her first visit to Givat Brenner:

Three years ago, when I was living in Jerusalem, I wrote Jessie a note: "I know your name. I should like to know you." She replied, telling me of the Rest Home and suggesting that I come to visit her there. I was in need of a holiday. I answered that I would come for a month.

It was November. I missed the last bus from Rehoboth and had to walk up from the road with my baggage. It was cold, dark and raining. I straggled up the steps of the Rest House, soaked to the bone. Leah hustled me into bed and brought hot tea. Then Jessie came and stood for a few moments at the threshold of the door. She said little beyond the accepted greeting. She wished me *"leil menuhah"* (a restful night).

I remember two things. The contour of her head in the doorway like a marble bust; and the eagerness of her unspoken questions. Who was I? What was I? Why was I? She seemed to have begun to probe me in those few seconds. She seemed feverishly impatient for the morning when we would really meet. I went to sleep thinking of the contour of that head; the softness of the eyes overshadowed by the strength of the thin lips. What manner of woman was this whom I had come to meet? Even in that night I sensed that here was an unusual life force.

In 1935, Jessie's sister and brother-in-law had come to see her — for ten days only, as Jessie was the sole reason of their coming and they were not interested in the country. Jessie's reaction is significant: "Then we must make the minutes count!" She got all the satisfaction she and Tamar needed out of this short visit. As the "Rest Home" was not quite ready to receive her guests, they visited Tel Aviv and Jerusalem together, stayed, much against Jessie's wishes, in the King David Hotel, and saw many old friends. But when the two sisters took leave of each other, they both had the feeling that they would not meet again in this life.

XVII

Struggle Against Illness

> . . . The less I can do other things, the
> more I write. I think I have an invisible
> task-master who won't let me do other
> things, so I should write.
>
> From a letter to her sister.

For a long time Jessie had been familiar with the
thought of death. Now she asked her sister to take care of
Tamar, and once more told her about her own last will and
testament, which had been in the hands of her friend and
lawyer, Mr. Israel Bar Shira, for many years. It would seem
that now and then in those years a peculiar sense of foreboding
came to Jessie. So she wrote in one of her letters the words
with which this chapter has been introduced.

In another letter Jessie tells her sister of her own varied
activities at Givat Brenner. She was asked to translate into
English, a Hebrew play about the illegal immigration. "It is
very tragic" she added.* She also taught English to the children
of Enzo Sereni, the guiding spirit of Givat Brenner, whom
she admired very much. And at the same time, she taught
Hebrew to some of the children from Germany, the new immigrants, and helped their parents to overcome the first difficulties of the new country. Moreover, she wrote some Yemenite stories in English and in Hebrew; one of them, "In

---

* I have not been able to find this play anywhere in Jessie's papers.

Memoriam," was published by *The Jewish Frontier* (March 1937) and offered a moving memorial sketch of a little hard-working Yemenite girl who died an early death. On the other hand, another story "The Servant Girl" was one of the very few humorous pieces that Jessie wrote. It brought her much acclaim when it was broadcast over the radio, much to the amusement of Jessie herself and of her friends at Givat Brenner (*Opinion,* March, 1938). Her "Comment on Antisemitism" had also been published by *Opinion* (February, 1938) and had brought her a prize. Well could she write on Valentine's Day, 1938:

> Even if the world is mad, my life is sane enough — fully occupied with work that is as absorbing as play. . . . I am writing all the time, the days fly . . . so beautiful, so quiet!

THE LAST DAYS

In March, 1938, she fell ill: an attack of pneumonia compelled her to go to the Hospital at Petah Tikvah, where she felt comfortable and was well taken care of. There the doctor told her that her normally strong heart was overstrained by the curvature of her spine, the after-effect of her early siege of infantile paralysis. He forbade her to do any physical labor, but she felt most reluctant to follow his advice and a little sad about it: "Why? I want to fuss around the garden and walk in the fields." Still, she had to confess that she had been "pretty ill."

Dorothy Kahn, who at that time returned to Givat Brenner, drawn by Jessie's magnetic charm, gives us a clear picture of her waning strength:

> For a while, our walks in the garden continued. Then, she was confined to the terrace. And finally, as her life was visibly fading, she was confined to her room. But restriction of movement could never touch the inner flame with which Jessie's body had nothing to do. Whether she could walk up and down the tree-lined paths or whether she was compelled to remain in her small bed,

Jessie walked over the world with her spirit. Everything mattered to her. Big things, little things. She could be as angry at me for forgetting to bring her the *"Yoman"* (the Hebrew journal of the *kvutzah*), as at some European statesman whom she believed to have acted stupidly. He mind and her spirit ground incenssantly like some mammoth mill. From behind the walls of her room — room number 7 — she reached out toward the world from which she was physically cut off.

Then, in the midst of their busy lives, both Jessie and Leah Berlin fell ill again in August, 1938, Jessie for the second time in one year. The blood test revealed malaria, and Jessie, with a guilty conscience, remembered that she had heard a mosquito buzzing in her bedroom, but had felt too lazy to get the "flit" and spray the obnoxious insect. Now Jessie confessed to her sister that, when first stricken, she felt as weak as in the almost forgotten childhood days, when she had first suffered from "infantile."

Gradually, both of them felt better; and Jessie had a special reason to get well in a hurry. Her 18 year old daughter Tamar had set her heart on a trip to America, but as Jessie had felt too weak for the journey, Tamar had gone on alone and had had a pleasant time with "Aunt Elvie" and all the other friends and relatives. Now Tamar was on her way back home to Givat Brenner, and Jessie was most anxious to have her daughter find her "wholly recuperated." "I was eager to have Tamar find me sound, so I decided not to die," she wrote to her sister . . . which goes to show that she felt how near the dark angel was to her. As to herself, she did not feel any fear of death. "It makes Life more beautiful not to fear the end of it." But anxious not to disappoint her young daughter, Jessie took good care of herself; she even had a trained nurse for some days, her usual remedy in times of bodily weakness.

"Now I feel grand!" she concluded her bulletin. In spite of this feeling, the malaria attack seems to have sapped what strength she had left, and poor Tamar was very much disappointed to find her mother in bed when she returned. Jessie's frail body, it seems, could not cope with the two serious illnesses of that year; her strength was failing.

Still, she kept on working. In July, she had sent a precious parcel to the United States, carefully wrapped in white sheeting. This was her novel, which she had started in 1922 and had revised and revised during more than ten years. At the same time, she finished the translation of Bialik's children's poems *Far Across The Sea*. This charming book was printed then and has appeared in several editions, since it has been a literary success as well as a book much beloved by children. Moreover, Jessie dedicated the last weeks of her life to her studies on Koheleth, which were published after her death, in Hebrew and English. With Dorothy Kahn she also collected her essays about the Kevutzah. They called this book *Collective* and tried to demonstrate in it the basic principles of the cooperative settlement. This book, her last manuscript, was taken to the bookbinder, wrapped and addressed in her usual orderly way, and sent to America some weeks before the end. Unfortunately, it seems to have been lost on its way to the States; it never turned up in Philadelphia. Finally, Jessie wrote some poems, in those last crowded weeks of her waning life, which seem to reveal her standing on "the threshold of another world." Last, but not least, Jessie Sampter gave her thoughts in those remaining moments of her life to an attempt at solving the problem of Arab-Jewish life in Palestine; *Ihud* (Unity) she called this study of a problem which may have very easily been in her mind when the last moment drew near.

In all those months of weakness, Jessie's poor wasted fingers had not lost their skill; when Hanukkah came, some weeks after her passing, the children of Givat Brenner received the games which their great friend had prepared for them with the same meticulous care that she gave to her studies on

Koheleth. The games were ready and waiting for them in Jessie's orderly closet.

"These last years were a crucible for Jessie," Dorothy Kahn tells us. "She saw all the things which were a part of the fabric of her life being torn to pieces. Her dream of peace seemed to be plunging toward a world conflict." All this may be true; we mentioned some of these dark forebodings earlier in this book. But from the weekly letters to her sister we also gather that there were happy moments — and whole days too! — in the course of these last months. In spite of her despair she knew full well that what had happened in the last twenty years, was one of the great events of the ages.

And right at the end, her eternally optimistic nature won out:

> Friendship . . . children . . . nature . . . books . . . work — there is healing for wounds (if not for scars) . . . .

Some plans about social work among Arabs and Jews brightened her last days. But this last year also brought her an intense longing for her sister; on Elvie's birthday, she had only one wish for her sister: that she might see her once more. In spite of this longing, she was not at all eager to go to America; she was "where she wanted to be" notwithstanding all the turmoil of the world. These words sum up all the contrast of these days:

> The world is so beautiful and men are so cruel! Two more Jews are murdered. . . . And Europe! . . . Oh what fragrance from the acacias. . . .

At last, the end came. "A strangely happy end" as her life-long friend, Mary Antin, termed it in a letter. In the last months, Jessie had been writing with a sort of feverish speed. Even when she was too weak to walk from her bed to the terrace, her pen never stopped. She herself was surprised at this speed; she took it as a favorable sign that she would be well again soon . . . (or did she?). "I am feeling much better" she added to her letter of October 10; and continued to "reach out for the world";

> How interesting it will be some day to read the history the world is now making!

In order to understand this same history better, she studied World History; she read Bryce's History of the Roman Empire as an introduction to Hitler's "Mein Kampf." It is a melancholy joy to know that her death prevented her from becoming acquainted with this document of barbarism. She saw President Roosevelt as a blessing to humanity, when he opened the doors of America to the immigrants. "You," so she told her sister, "are living in the safest and sanest of countries. But I don't envy you." And proudly she informed her correspondents that, in spite of all the trouble, creative activity had never ceased in Palestine:

> Thirty new settlements have been started!
> My days are full, though quiet, and creative in their activity. Writing; young and old people to teach or to "have talks with"; some friendship and a little personal love; garden; misunderstandings to be understood; people coming and going; and enough silence and being alone. So Life goes along, doing what is its business to do — clarifying itself more and more, despite the very deep dip down that the world is making just now. . . .

"I am feeling very well now." These are the last words in the last letter which she wrote to her sister (November 11, 1938). On Friday morning, she said goodbye, in high spirits, to her friend Leah Berlin to go to the hospital in Petah Tikvah for a checkup. Two hours later she was dead.

They brought her home to Givat Brenner on Sunday; the small black coffin was decorated by Jessie's friend, Esther, the gardener, to whom she had dedicated one of her last poems, and by Leah Berlin, with the white chrysanthemums which Jessie had planted and tended herself. At the foot of the coffin stood the two small candlesticks made of olive wood, which had been used by Jessie on many a Friday night to kindle her Sabbath lights. This was Jessie's Sabbath now, after a life of toil and constant quest. The serenity and simple beauty of her funeral on Tuesday seemed almost like a symbol of that serene "Sabbath soul" *(neshamah yeterah)* which had helped her to overcome all the troubles of her life, while still retaining her peace of mind.

An eyewitness, Julia Dushkin, has given us a moving account of this unforgettable burial. In the *Beth Hatarbuth* (Lecture Room) of the settlement, stood Jessie's coffin covered with garlands of flowers brought by the Yemenite children whom Jessie had loved and who had lost their best friend. On a low stool near the table there burned the two tiny candles. Four stalwart workmen lifted the coffin, carried it out on the green lawn and set it down under a flowering acacia tree. The mourners were a strange mixture of immigrants from all the four corners of the world: members of the *kibbutz,* parents, children, and new little immigrants from Germany, saved from the holocaust. Jessie had taught them their first Hebrew words. Four people spoke at Jessie's bier: a laborer from Rehoboth, one from the *kibbutz* Givat Brenner, Leah and Miss Szold. So still was the air that it was as if only the animals and birds had voices, when from afar came the lowing of a cow or the cackling of a hen.

Then they lowered her carefully and gently into the freshly dug grave. The fathers of some of her comrades chanted the Kaddish and one of them entreated her soul to be the instrument for sending peace to the troubled earth. Miss Szold threw the first shovel of freshly dug loam; then followed the workmen. What an extraordinary *Chevrah Kadishah!* When it was Leah's turn to throw her armful of flowers, she murmured: *"Numi kezat, Jessie!* (Rest awhile, Jessie!) as she had often said to her friend, when Jessie was tired out.

When all seemed over, it was not over for Miss Szold.
Quickly she went back to the *Beth Hatarbuth*. There were the
boys and girls of the Youth Aliyah in their clean shirts and
white blouses. "Shalom!" they greeted her. Then Miss Szold
sat down in their midst and told them about the friend they
all had lost: the dramatic story of her life, and how she had
freed herself from the bondage of her crippled body; how,
through internationalism, she had come to Jewish nationalism;
how she came to Palestine and to Labor Zionism in Givat
Brenner. Zionism could best be served by following in Jessie
Sampter's footsteps. Thus Miss Szold, on the very day of Jessie
Sampter's funeral, planted the first seeds of Jessie's life after
death.

Not long before, two comrades of the *kibbutz* had been
carried out to the little graveyard of Givat Brenner. On this
occasion Jessie had written her last Hebrew song — perhaps
feeling that it would be her turn soon. I have tried to translate
her Hebrew words into English.

On The Slope Of The Hill
(*Bemorad Hahar*)

The "House of Life" is waiting
There on the slope of the hill.
Who knows, today, if not tomorrow
Sleep there he will.

It is wonderful to be resting
Beneath the radiant sky,
Where the sun sings his song to the mountains,
And the birds pour out their cry.

Some morn, from my narrow bedstead
Arise I also will.
And then I shall sleep in the evening
There . . . on the slope of the hill.

─────────────XVIII

Ingathering

> O Thou that hast with vision filled my
> soul
> And made my speech and deed inadequate;
> Forgive my crudeness, my unripe desires,
> Foolhardy courage, childish fearlessness. . . .
>
> *Homing*

"The Ingathering of the Exiles" (*Kibbutz Galuyoth*) has become a current term for what is at the same time the proudest achievement and the hardest problem of the young State of Israel. Jessie Sampter had another kind of "ingathering" in mind when she repeatedly called her poems "The Ingathering." It was the harvest, the "Ingathering" of her poetical life during more than thirty years, a running commentary on her actual life, as she termed her poetry, in the Introduction to her collected poems, *Brand Plucked From The Fire*. And now, after we have looked at the physical life of this courageous woman, which started in the spacious Sampter Mansion on Fifth Avenue in New York and ended in the plain "Room No. 7" at Givat Brenner in Palestine, it is fitting to look at this Ingathering and ask: What was the impact of Jessie Sampter's poetry on her contemporaries? What was its relation to the work of her fellow poets? How did the critics receive her book? And do her songs live on today or are they forgotten?

JESSIE'S POETRY AND THE CRITICS

First of all, we shall have to look at the contents of her *Brand Plucked From The Fire*. The title, itself, seems to indicate that many of these poems were born in the fiery distress of her life. She divided them into five groups. The first contained the songs about the "Land of Israel," and treated all the different aspects of the old-new land and of its returned children. Of similar importance is the last group, called "Diaspora." Jessie Sampter saw her life as a bridge between the Diaspora and Israel.

It is an interesting experience to examine the critical reviews of her poems. It is gratifying to see that most of them were favorable; they express the gratitude of Jews all over the world to this warm-hearted spokesman of their people. Ralph Marcus held that the air of Palestine, which, according to the saying of our fathers, makes a man wise, had deepened and ripened Jessie's own inherent wisdom. But much more can be learned from the carping critics than from this praise. It is significant that the extreme right and the extreme left in American Jewry found it difficult to appreciate this poetry. There is the rabbi from Louisville who, though he concedes that "Miss Sampter was that '*rara avis*' an American Zionist who came to Palestine to *live* there," also severely blamed her for being an 'agnostic'; it may have seemed to him — according to her "Confession" in *The Reconstructionist* (Vol. III, Nos. 3-4) — that she "saw in Zionism a new substitute for religion." Publishers and readers will not bother "to burn their hands with smoky brands" he concludes somewhat spitefully. While this critic overlooked the deep longing for a religious rebirth in the Holy Land, which is quite as explicit in her poetry as in her "Confession," the radical Yiddish newspaper *Freiheit* blamed the poet for preaching "a poetry of submission," and missed "revolt and uproar" in her songs. "It is Zionist poetry for Diaspora readers." Perhaps the author herself would not have been dissatisfied with this verdict.

Most of her critics stress the importance of her religious poems, "Psalms in Struggle," which were written long before she ever set foot in Palestine. They portray Jessie's constant quest for God, for a religion, for a congregation which she could join in prayer. These are poems which reveal in her the makings of a genuine religious poet, show her as the descendant of Shlomo ibn Gabirol and Yehudah HaLevi. It is true that, in the Palestine poems, this quest for God is somewhat hidden behind the mercy of the "return," the new religion of working the soil of the old-new homeland, as Jessie had expressed it years ago in her poem "Return";

> "And when our eyes behold again
> Thy mercy over Zion reign,
> How wilt Thou come? what shall we see?
> We'll see a plowman plow for corn
> Beneath the newly risen morn. . . ."

However, as we have seen already in her first years in Palestine, Jessie knew that this blessed relief was not enough and she longed for the religious renascence which, to the last day of her life, she hoped to see.

Taking them all in all most of the critics (with the exception of the rabbi from Louisville) appreciate the deep religious feeling which seems to derive its inspiration from the Book of Psalms, as well as from modern poets like Sara Teasdale and Walt Whitman. They also praise the simple Canterbury Tales-like quality of her everyday chronicles from Palestine. The limitations of the poetry are seen in the all too readily idyllic style, and in the metre which now and then lapses into jingles.

It is easy to understand why these "jingles" were written: Jessie was an educator as well as a poet, and she wanted the children in America, as well as Jewish children all over the world, to read and to like these poems which introduced them to Jewish customs, to Jewish history and to Jewish rebirth in Palestine. It is her greatest achievement that the critic of the New York Herald Tribune thought that he "could smell the freshly turned earth of Palestine and see visions of strong muscular men and women" in Jessie's pictures of life in Palestine. That is what she would have wanted to convey. More than one critic felt that "the author is greater than any song she wrote; a much greater poem would be an account of her life's history . . . but that she cannot write herself." That is the reason why this book was written.

It is a bit disappointing to find that hardly any one of her critics was aware of the new phase her poetry seemed to enter in the last decades of her life. Perhaps this is none of their fault, since they had access only to the poems published in *Brand Plucked From The Fire*. They were not familiar with the development of Jessie's poetry in her later years. The great discovery of the "new poetry" by the American poets of the first two decades of this century, which saw the emergence of the "Imagists" and the free verse poets, did not fail to leave its mark on the poetry of Jessie Sampter, whose small room in Givat Brenner contained on its shelves some of the American and English poets whom she delighted to read. The Imagists, in 1919, had defined their aims in poetry by stressing that henceforth "they would use the language of common speech" in their free verse pictures of modern life. No longer would they copy ancient rhythms, but instead would express themselves in free verse to symbolize their freedom of thought. Hilda Doolittle and Amy Lowell strove for the same "artistic value of modern life" that Jessie Sampter wanted to portray in her *Emek*. Here, and in her last songs (written after *Brand* came out) Jessie abandoned her old, facile and sometimes almost "jingly" verse for the hard and clear pictures of harsh reality seen through the eyes of the living poet. Frost pictured New England life and Masters portrayed the men of Spoon River with the same relentless realism that Jessie Sampter brought to bear on her Palestine poems. It is with this new poetic law in mind that we must look at Jessie's new poetry, her *Emek* and her last poems. We shall find that she succeeded in giving us the lifelike portraits of the new settlers in ancient Palestine. These are the men and women who are toiling, plowing, harvesting and playing there. Some of the *kevutzot* may look different today, it is true, but their basic aspects and problems are the same. And nobody brought out those aspects with the same strength and relentlessness as this clear-sighted woman who travelled through the Emek in 1925. There is "Resurrection," the lone woman-farmer, and "Ben Brak" and all the children in their nurseries and schools — the whole "army of peace" who still bring the message of Israeli youth to their brethren in the Diaspora, just as the "Valley of Youth" brought it in the days of Jessie Sampter.

Some of Jessie's critics in 1937 did not overlook another no less eloquent message of her poetry: its last words:

"Poor poets that in agonies of speech
strive for the silences they cannot reach!"

It seems as if Jessie had tried in her last poems to reach out to these very same "silences." They are strange, sometimes mysterious, and have a peculiar lilting charm which you find in the poems of Emily Dickinson. As I already mentioned, Jessie sent them to her cousin and friend, Professor Louis Wise. Some of them (not all) were published by *Opinion*. Her last poem, written only some weeks before she died in November 1938, was called *"That"* and tried to express just that unspeakable mystery which all beings dream of and which nobody can express . . . the "Unknown." It seems to the reader

that, in this poem, with its halting, slowly increasing rhythm,
the poet is herself standing on tiptoe . . . on the threshold of
another world.

THE PROSE WRITINGS OF JESSIE SAMPTER

Though Jessie Sampter's prose writings cover much more
space than her poetical work, she thought of herself as essen-
tially a poet, and considered her journalistic contributions as a
duty that had to be performed because she had promised to
do it, or because she felt the urgent necessity of bearing "Testimony." We remember that it was her journalistic mission as
reporter to Hadassah and the Z. O. A. which offered the
only opportunity available for her obtaining a visa for
Palestine.

Her prose writings are of various types; all of them are educational. To this group belong her admirable Zionist text
books, which helped to educate a whole generation of American youth in Zionism. A second group is constituted by her
journalistic reports written after she came to Palestine in 1919.
In a very interesting letter, Miss Szold told Jessie's sister how
conscientiously Jessie took this task to heart; she felt as if she
did not deserve her position as a reporter, because her pen
could not keep up with the overwhelming impressions of her
first weeks in Eretz Yisrael.

Jessie Sampter's articles are to be found in most of the early
Zionist magazines: the *Hadassah Bulletin,* the *Maccabean,* the
Young Judaean, the *New Palestine.* Later on, she also wrote
for the *Menorah Journal,* the *Jewish Frontier,* the *Jewish
Review, The Reconstructionist* and *Opinion.*

Again, it is the educator in Jessie Sampter who writes most
of these stories and articles. Her stories in the *Young Judaean*
are to be seen in this context. After coming to Palestine, she
tried, in a series of reports which she called "Miriam's Journal," to introduce the young readers of the *Young Judaean*

to the beauties and the different localities of the Holy Land.*
In fact, in writing these first articles, she may have thought of
her own nephew and niece, Edgar and Jessie, whom she wanted
to read these articles instead of a letter from their "Auntie
Jessie," as she often mentions in her letters.

Long before her own *aliyah,* she had tried, in numerous
articles in the *Maccabean* and the *Young Judaean* and in her
poems for the Jewish child, to communicate the Zionist message to Jewish children. There would be no point in enumerat-
ing all her articles here; only some of her most poignant efforts
shall be mentioned.

All of the articles seem to aim at a sober, efficient style of
writing, in fact, at the very qualities that we would like to see
in a journalist. It is significant that, as soon as Jessie was moved
by a special emotion or her heart was all too full of her Jewish
people, her prose gave way to poetry. So many of the poems
which we later on find in her book of poetry, *The Coming of
Peace,* were born in this way. For instance, the moving poem
"Victory" (*Maccabaean,* June, 1918) tells the Biblical story of
David and Absalom once more, the triumph of the soldiers,
and at the same time the grief of the victorious father whose
victory meant the loss of his son:

"I shall eat but dust and ashes, dust and ashes, dust and ashes
    In the streets of Zion town. . . ."

It would seem as if Jessie Sampter had revealed in these
unassuming words, the secret of every military victory; there is
always somebody who has to eat "dust and ashes," because he
has lost his dearest treasure, while the soldiers are celebrating
their victory. That is how Jessie felt about the glory of war.
Instead of writing about this theme, she retold the story of
David and Absalom, and made it a symbol of every victory
gained by war — the essence of war itself.

---

* *Young Judaean,* December, 1919; April, 1920; November, 1920; December,
1920.

After she came to Palestine, her journalistic aims were primarily to report on the situation in Palestine — good or bad — as the case might be. In consequence of these reports, her articles in the *New Palestine* did not fail to mention the "Errors in Utopia," the plight of the Yemenites and the lack of religious fervor which she had experienced in Jerusalem soon after her arrival. On the other hand, she faithfully and happily reported the "glad tidings," wherever they appeared. So her "'Twentieth Century Legends" deal with the coming to Jerusalem of Sir Herbert Samuel and his being greeted by many of the believers as a forerunner of the Messiah (*Young Judaean,* March, 1921).

There was a second aim in her mind, when she wrote these articles, and this was even closer to her heart. She wanted to call upon American youth to follow her own example and "to be counted," to become pioneers, as their own ancestors had been when they built up America. To "The Never Starters and the Quitters" she addressed her appeal in moving words (*New Palestine,* June 23, 1922):

> ... Go for a visit; then, afterwards, you will want to stay. Or, if you do not, you shall not sleep in peace, the still, small voice will call you reproachfully night and day. ...
> The urge of your heart and the compunction of your conscience will give you no rest. Dare you go for a visit? Ask those who have been to Palestine and returned, the happy, unhappy Americans who went to Palestine to leave. ...

Today, American tourists in Palestine view with pride and admiration the numerous American colonies in Israel, where American boys and girls unite the know-how of their native land with the enthusiasm the Jewish pioneers: Ein Hashofet (The Well of the Judge), named after Judge Brandeis is one of the earliest; in recent years, Gesher Haziv, Yiftah, S'doth Mordekhai, Urim, Sassa and many more have come into being. Perhaps these modern guests ought not to forget that it was a frail woman from New York who kindled in many of these American youths the flame of enthusiasm which inspired them, as it had her, to live in Palestine and to build up the land.

In her later years in Palestine, Jessie Sampter took it upon herself to deal with specific problems of the Yishuv and of Palestinian youth. Again, the Yemenite problem is never silent in her heart; so she sent to the *Jewish Frontier* (November, 1936) the moving story of the little working girl, Saida, who became a victim of her early upbringing: eight years old, she had to work and help to support her family, while her father studied the "Holy Books" and let his three wives and his children work for him ("In Memoriam to a Working Girl").

An episode from the times of the Arab riots deals with defense problems. "Revenge" is the story of a brother who wants to avenge his dearest friend and — kills his sister (*Jewish Frontier*, March, 1938). And "Watchwomen" pays due tribute and admiration to the group of brave women who were the first pioneer working women in Palestine: Maya Wilbushewitz, Rachel Jannait, Leah Berlin (*Jewish Frontier*, November, 1936).

These moving and well-written stories and articles occupied Jessie Sampter during the last years of her life. But a peculiar sort of "Epilogue" was granted to her, when, in 1940, quite a while after she herself had gone to her eternal rest, *Opinion* published some new Palestinian portraits of hers, which were again illustrated by Ruth Light-Kazmann as her earlier Palestinian portraits had been. These significant poems, as well as the two treatises on Koheleth, which were published posthumously both in Palestine and in America call for separate treatment. We shall speak about them in the next chapter.

XIX

Afterglow

He sings: "To wait is certainty,
For time is never done,
And he who lives a splendid hour,
A deathless hour has won."

He stands upon my soul and whips
My white doves toward the sky,
And sings: "T'is glorious to live
And wonderful to die."

Fairy and Angel

It may have seemed to Jessie as though she were writing a sequel to her collection of Palestinian Portraits contained in the *Emek,* when several years later, after she had moved to Givat Brenner, she felt impelled to write the poems which she called "Ingathering." They were published in 1934 and were superbly illustrated by her friend and erstwhile neighbor from Rehoboth, Ruth Light-Kazmann.

More Palestinian Portraits

They are a series of four poems which all deal with the problems of the Halutzim; in fact, each of these poems seems to represent a peculiar type of Halutz, and, taken together, they give an abbreviated history of the immigration to Palestine during these decades. There is, first of all, Sara, the Halutzah from Russia, who came to find peace in labor and fellowship, but cannot find it because her heart is too full of memories:

"We bring our restlessness to rest in the land
We dance with frantic joy, sing with longing and
   determination
But we cannot sleep without dreams.
It will be different with our children
They will have been born in this still land
They will have sucked their thoughts from its
   silence
They will have plowed quietly above the
   earthquake.
Pastured with sheep from infancy among the
   thorns and the lilies
They will know peace."

The second poem in this series shows Deborah, daughter of Miriam and Joseph, born in Daganiah. Deborah seems to give her own answer to the problem of Sara, the Halutzah from Russia. She "moves with the grace and fulness of boughs in the wind. . . ." The heroes of the Bible "were her playmates and school companions."

But not all the families of the Halutzim have problems that are as easily solved as Deborah's. There is the "Kurdistan Woman," who lives in a cave-like house in Tiberias and "passes quietly along the way of her people." She has found her own solution. From a totally different world comes "Sydney, now Shakneh," a successful lawyer from Boston, Massachusetts. But he did not appreciate his success and came to the free commune of labor with his wife and children to live a life of freedom and work:

"And here they are,
And here they stay."

Sydney is the typical Halutz from America, whom Jessie

Sampter had called upon in her urgent articles in the *New Palestine*. He seems like an answer to her prayer.

It is indeed a colorful assembly which got together in the homeland, and we can understand that Jessie, who "loved people" was fascinated, in more than one way. In 1935, she added to her portraits two more, which reveal another phase and another layer of the immigration. There is Kadia, the young mother, whom we have already met in Jessie's own life as her disciple, her friend and helper. She was born in a village in Palestine to parents who came from Yemen and represents the outcome of Jessie's own work for the Yemenite women and children. Kadia and the Hasid, born in Tiberias to Polish parents, are the redeemed generation and will live a life of freedom and work, while they might have withered away in the hovels of Yemen and Poland, if Zion had not saved their souls.

These "portraits" might have represented a sort of testament of Jessie Sampter's: they all live by the strength of Jessie's own achievements in Palestine. But as we already mentioned, something like an "Afterglow" appeared to keep her memory green, long after she had gone to sleep "on the slope of the hill." In 1940, four more "Palestinian Portraits" were published; and they seem to me the most significant of the whole series. For they bind the old to the new, and they bring the hearts of the parents near to the hearts of the children. There are the "Baby Rabbi," who plays in the sunlight of Palestine, the full-grown man from Jerusalem, who studied in Italy and returned to his mother-land, to Palestine. There is Jessie's own beloved daughter "Tamar," "this young daughter of Israel, fed on milk and honey and figs and grapes." The last portrait is the most appealing of all; it is that of a *"lamed-vavnik,"* one of the thirty-six holy men whose identity is unknown, but whose merit is enough to save the world:

"He feeds creatures of want older than he, poorer than he
With the loaves of bread
Bought with the pence of his begging. . . ."

This man would seem to portray Jessie's own ideal of loving
kindness, turning up behind the mask of an old beggar in
Jerusalem.

KOHELETH

Dorothy Kahn, as we saw, wrote that, in her last days in
Givat Brenner, Jessie Sampter, ailing though she might have
been, was feverishly busy with her studies on Koheleth, the
Biblical preacher of vanity:

> About this same time, she was reading Koheleth with me.
> Although she was as pedantic as usual about pointing out the
> verb constructions and the word derivations — I sensed that it
> was difficult for her to restrict her mind to my Hebrew lesson.
> An idea which she had had for several years was being crystal-
> lized. For a month afterwards, she worked unceasingly on a
> philosophic treatise on Koheleth, in which she sets out to
> show the similarities between the teachings of the Preacher and
> those of the *kibbutzim*. These hundred pages — in her painful
> scrawl! — with words and phrases crossed out, and margins filled
> with notes, are now being typed.

Where are "these hundred pages" which Jessie wrote down
with her last strength? We do not know if this "labor of love"
has been preserved in its entirety; but we are fortunate enough
to have two editions of Jessie Sampter's Koheleth dialogues,
one in Hebrew and one in English. In the very fine illustrated
booklet which was brought out in Givat Brenner, after Jessie's
death, we find a Koheleth-Dialogue in Hebrew; the Introduction tells us that it is translated from the English original
which was later found in Jessie's papers. This is a very vivid
discussion between a novel Koheleth, who seems to live in
Palestine and is at the same time the Ancient Sage, and a

young friend and critic of his. Another of these dialogues was
printed in *The Reconstructionist,* in 1940 (January 5, 1940).
It would, indeed, have been a pity if these colorful dialogues
had not been saved for us. For they contain, though not
exactly a philosophical treatise as Dorothy Kahn wrote, some
vivid pictures from the new life in Palestine, together with an
extract from the wisdom of the ancient sage who came back to
the world to live in Palestine. In an easy, readable manner
these dialogues give us the extract of Jessie's life philosophy
and that of Koheleth, as she saw him. She assumes that the
ancient sage took the name of Shelomo, the King, to make his
words more impressive to the people.

In summing up the value of Jessie Sampter's Koheleth
dialogues we see that they do not give us any startling new
scholarly discoveries about the ancient Biblical hero, but they
succeed in regrouping his thoughts as given in the original
book of Koheleth in such a skillful manner that, at the end,
the ancient prophet of the vanity of life and the denyer of
every human endeavor is compelled to come out into the open
as an advocate of the life in the cooperative settlements in
Palestine, and, moreover, as an apostle of Jessie's own dearly-
bought wisdom of living life and whatever happens in life.
As Goethe's Faust, after he had drunk the love-potion, "saw
Helena in every woman," so Jessie Sampter became so enthusiastic over the *kibbutz* philosophy, that, in every sage she
encountered, in Krishna Murti as well as in Koheleth, she
discovered the theory of *kibbutz* life. "Enjoy your share in life
in spite of all your trouble; but do not take for yourself *more
than your share!*"

These are the final words of her Hebrew Koheleth dialogue
in the "Yesha" book of Givat Brenner. *The Reconstructionist*
Koheleth tries to answer the questions of the "friend and
critic" in a more humorous vein and stresses the sentence —
also contained in Koheleth — that "the young man should

rejoice in his youth and walk in the ways of his heart and find
happiness in his work." Not moved by any illusion about the
character and the worth of human endeavor, Koheleth knows
that life is full of pain and man is often full of greed and ambition. Koheleth knows this and Jessie Sampter knows it, too.
But both of them agree that the very fact of impending death
should move us to savor life all the more. The Biblical
Koheleth paradoxically concluded his gloomy thoughts with
a surprising turn to religion. "All is contained in the fear of
God, and this is the basis of life." However, Jessie Sampter,
who in her later years "did not want to utter the name of God
in vain," replaces this surprising turn to God with her turn to
"life and work." She conquered her own pessimism with the
slogan, "Life is good after all, for it allows us to work." This
was A. D. Gordon's message to the workmen of Palestine; this
was Jessie Sampter's last message, too, as embodied in her
Koheleth dialogues.

In the end, it is no longer Koheleth being re-interpreted,
but Jessie Sampter conveying to the reader her dearly bought
philosophy of life; and this is what makes these dialogues so
valuable for us. They are Jessie Sampter's testament to the
world.

Shut the book, and you will see an image of the rugged,
wrinkled philosopher and sage with his white mane and
strong teeth, reclining in the shade of an olive tree and letting his keen eyes wander from the young pine trees, gently
moved by the breeze over the sand dunes, to the blue sea on
the far horizon. This is a miniature portrait of Palestine
scenery which Jessie, the inveterate lover of Palestine, wanted
to convey in these dialogues along with the wisdom of Koheleth.

IN THE BEGINNING

However, the wisdom of a renewed Koheleth did not re-

main the last word of Jessie Sampter's. In 1953, fifteen years
after her passing, a whole unknown book of hers came out
into the open. This is her three-volume novel "In the Beginning." Never published before, this book makes you feel
that Jessie Sampter is indeed alive and as full of timely questions as she was fifteen years ago.

This is the book which Jessie, as her letters told us, started
to write in a moment of deep distress in 1921. After finishing
the first draft she revised it again and again for more than
ten years. In fact, as long as she lived, she never tired of
coming back to it. At last she sent the manuscript to America,
carefully wrapped in sheets, as was her orderly way. Jessie's
clever friends, Edith Eder, the psychoanalyst, and Leah Berlin,
the manager of Beth Yesha, had read its first chapters and both
agreed that it was going to be a great book, if Jessie went on
as she had begun. The author herself seems to have valued this
book more than any of her other efforts. She asked her sister
to cable her as soon as she received the precious freight, and
she was happy to know that this manuscript, after her own
death, would be kept in "the safest and sanest of countries."

Still, this book would have been destroyed if Jessie's devoted
sister could have brought herself to destroy something written
by Jessie. For like the common-sense American that lived in
Jessie's soul alongside of the poet in her, she had uttered the
wish that whatever of her manuscripts was not published
five years after her own death, should be destroyed. However,
Jessie's sister, like many another friend of a deceased author,
(the most famous of all these manuscript-savers was no other
than Emperor Augustus who rescued Vergil's Aeneid from
oblivion), also decided to hold the manuscript; and so she
saved for us a most revealing account of Jessie's own "spiritual
biography," and at the same time a vivid chronicle of a little
known phase in the history of American Zionism.

In the Beginning is the dramatic life story of a young

American girl, Evelyn Frieden, who grew up in a "well-regu-
lated American home" just like the author herself. Here too,
Christmas trees and Easter eggs replaced Hanukkah candles
and Passover, and the little girl is helplessly amazed when
she encounters anti-Semitism for the first time in her life.
She even denies being Jewish, as Jessie herself did in her
early childhood, and afterwards tries with all her might to
correct her statement, because the children might think "that
she had told them a lie." In spite of loving parents and a big
family, the little girl is not at all happy and does not feel
secure; sometimes she is near suicidal ideas. Only once in her
short life did she feel "safe and wonderful;" that happened
when she "saw the stars," by the merest chance, not in her
shade-protected nursery, but in travelling to their summer
cottage, when they had to wait for a train at night. This unique
feeling did not come back to her, and in growing up, Evelyn
looked everywhere in vain for a community, which she might
join in prayer, and so recover this lost feeling of security. All
the children felt that they "are not anything" and did not belong to any religious group. Evelyn's sister, with this same restlessness, turned to Unitarianism for a while. Her older brother
married a Gentile girl, true to his father's education, and
forgot all about his Jewish faith — all the more easily since
they changed their name "Frieden" to "Freeman," which did
not sound so "outlandish." Evelyn herself experienced a
"miracle," as she called it in her heart; she discovered the
beauty and dignity of Jewish customs and symbols. A school-
fellow of hers invited her to her own home, where Jewish
tradition was alive; and Evelyn was so carried away that she
tried to live the life of an observant Jew herself. Misunder-
standing and mockery in her own family-circle made her resolve to run away. She took a business course to become independent financially and then moved to the Young Women's
Hebrew Association in order to learn more about her Jewish

people. Here she began to study Hebrew with a group of other
girls, and the rabbinical student Emanuel Perski, who taught
her group, became her first lover, as he seemed to share her
own enthusiasm and ideals.

War came to America, and Evelyn's older brother, the beloved companion of her childhood, was killed in France.
Evelyn, though deeply distressed by his death, remained steadfast and dedicated to her dream of Zionism, which, she felt
would be the only way to redeem the homeless Jews and,
through them, to redeem all mankind. As soon as there was
the slightest chance, she left her native land for Palestine,
though her lover Emanuel did not accompany her, as he
wanted to get his degree first in order to be better equipped
for service.

However, deep disappointment awaited Evelyn in Palestine.
She loved the land, the balmy air, the scenery, the history
and the old-new language. But she was cruelly disappointed
in its inhabitants. There was no leader in Palestine, nor was
there the Messianic vision which American Zionists had hoped
to find there. In the Holy City Evelyn did not find a congregation which she might join in prayer; the Oriental Jews
did not allow women to pray with the men, which offended
Evelyn's feeling of dignity, and the modern Jews did not
pray at all. Moreover, Evelyn could not overlook the fact that
there were "errors in Utopia:" the earlier settlers exploited
and mistreated the newcomers from Yemen, those devout pil-
grims who had come through the desert to reach the borders of
the Holy Land. Their little girls and their women were poorly
paid servants of the settlers, while their men sat at home and
studied the Talmud. Evelyn was again near to despair and
longed for death to escape from her "God who failed."

Slowly she found the way to her own task. When she had
left America, a friend of her family, an ardent Zionist, Boaz,

who was himself a farmer and engineer, had strongly objected
to her going to Palestine as a stenographer. "Why don't you
go to work in the vineyards and orchards?" "That is what
Zionists should do!" Now this same Boaz lived in Rehoboth
and hired her to work in his own vineyard. Moreover, he
introduced her to the *Havurah,* the community of workers
where Hava Shalom, as Evelyn was called in Palestine, found
her own dreams of a new form of society realized. No "ready
made cash" was offered to anybody, as it had been to her in
her childhood. Everybody worked and earned as much as he
needed to live. Hava joined this cooperative settlement and
felt deeply satisfied, though, on the way to her goal, she lost
her lover, Emanuel. The young rabbi preferred a comfortable
congregation in America to the austere life of a pioneer in
Palestine.

Fulfillment came at long last to Hava Shalom, when she
met another man, a bearded young immigrant from Russia,
Nahman ben David. He is "the man to whom she belongs
and who belongs to her." But here, too, the way to their final
marriage was not easy; Nahman had to fight his way from an
over-orthodox education and an early misguided marriage,
to a worker's community in Palestine. Even now he could
not offer her an "honorable marriage," as his wife in Russia
was alive but could not be reached for divorce. In spite of
these obstacles they were united; for they felt that they shared
the same ideas and ideals, the same outlook on "the stars."
Both of them understood that the ancient wisdom of Judaism
revealed all the wisdom there is. "Love your neighbor, he is
like you!" as Jessie Sampter — Hava Shalom — translated the
age-old command. This wisdom applied to the Arab as well as
the Jew. In a symbolic action Nahman ben David broke the
pistol of his Arab adversary in two; each of the two adversaries
kept one half, "for half a pistol cannot harm anybody." "When

you love your neighbor as yourself, you know what God is,"
this is Nahman's final word, and it is Jessie Sampter's message as needed today as it was in her lifetime.

"Here in Palestine, with her husband, Hava was overjoyed
to reap the "first harvest" of all her efforts when her child was
born. Through thousands of years of longing they came back
to Creation, to the "Beginning."

There are the makings of a great book in this all-too-long-
hidden autobiographical novel of Jessie Sampter's, though the
book, itself, is far from perfection. Still, it ought to be published; for it clearly describes the hard way of early American
Zionism and the strength of the message which was destined
to save many thousands of Jewish souls in the time of catastrophe.

Jessie Sampter's message of peace in Israel, as we all know,
has not to this day (1956), been fulfilled. In fact, we seem
to be further removed from its final goal than during her life.
But it will have to be fulfilled before the State of Israel can
be said to have realized the expectations of its founders. So
Jessie Sampter, the poet, becomes, in this novel, a Jewish
prophetess in her own right — not, like Deborah, the herald
of battle and victory, but a herald of peace between neighbors,
and of peace all over the world.

XX

Is Jessie Sampter Alive Today?

> Frail is my taper; it flickers in the wind
> It is blown out in the great wind of the
> world.
>
> Yet when the world is dead and the seas are
> a crust of salt
> When the sun is dark in heaven and the
> stars have changed their courses,
> Forever somewhere with Thee, on the altar
> of life
> Shall still be burning the white fire of my
> heart.
> *White Fire*

Is Jessie Sampter and her poetry still remembered today? That the "dead do not die" was one of the main convictions of her life and her philosophy; in what sense, then, does this apply to herself?

At first, one is tempted to deny that this shy, peace-loving woman and her sensitive poetry are still a living force in the State of Israel or in her native land. Did not history by-pass her peaceful dreams of Ishmael and Isaac, living fraternally side by side in Palestine? However, on second thought, we cannot but see that the seeds which Miss Szold had planted on the day of Jessie's burial did not wither but have blossomed and borne fruit. In fact, Jessie Sampter's name has become a "legend" in Israel, as some of her friends told me; and here, in America, she has also become a living force in the way she would have wished to be.

After the impressive burial "on the slope of the hill," Jessie was sadly missed at Givat Brenner, as Dorothy Kahn told us. She and Leah Berlin felt "lost without Jessie." When the *sheloshim,* the first thirty days of mourning were over, the "comrades" of the *kibbutz* decided to edit a well-selected booklet *Yesha Sampter Leyom Hasheloshim,* which we already mentioned and which contained the Hebrew translation of Jessie's Koheleth-dialogues. This booklet has proved more valuable than the Editors could know for keeping Jessie's thoughts alive, for it contained not only several very significant pictures of Jessie's, but also the Hebrew translation of ten of her Aphorisms, which she wrote in the last years of her life. These Aphorisms, which she called "Interpretations," were sent to America along with her letters and, unfortunately, seem to have been lost on the way. Mrs. Wachenheim, who with meticulous care, preserved every scrap of paper written by her sister, has not been able to discover them among Jessie's papers. So the ten "Aphorisms" in the Hebrew Memorial Book are the last remnants of these "Interpretations," which Jessie herself valued highly and often in her letters called the "Testament" and the summing up of her life's thought. To give a general idea of their contents, here are the titles of the ten Aphorisms salvaged by the Memorial Book of Givat Brenner:

1. No words (can tell it)
2. My room
3. Give me a neighbor
4. Knowledge of good
5. The birth
6. The God of the cats
7. Fear of loneliness
8. Result
9. Life in our days
10. When the bombs thundered

After some time, Miss Szold did her share to keep Jessie's

memory alive. It seems that she had promised to write an introduction to a Hebrew translation of the *Book of the Nations*. But this plan came to naught. Instead, something more fruitful was performed. After some years, the young Palestinian writer, Pinchas Lender, a gifted journalist and contributor to *Ha-aretz,* the leading Palestine newspaper, translated Jessie's poetry into a clear and lucid Hebrew. A miniature booklet was printed by *Ahdut,* the Cooperative Publishing Company in Tel Aviv. The original name in Hebrew, *Ud Mutzal Me-Esh,* was preserved, and several pieces from the *Emek* were added. This little book is a real gem and ought to be widely distributed as a gift to all friends of Hebrew poetry and of Jessie Sampter. Some of her poems read as if they were only now returned to their mother-tongue. Miss Szold had written the Introduction in Hebrew and told her readers what she had told the children of Givat Brenner after Jessie's burial, the story of Jessie's dedicated life.

In Jessie's native America, there was a different sort of survival. There is hardly a modern Reform Prayer Book or Collection of Hymns for Jewish children that does not include one or several poems by her. In fact, this may have been a little detrimental to her memory among American readers; they only know Jessie Sampter as a children's poet and an authority for Sunday School programs. When the Central Conference of American Rabbis met in 1951 and decided to re-edit the Union Hymnal they chose three poems from Jessie Sampter's *Around the Year* and set them to music. At Passover, the new Manischewitz Haggadah reprinted her "Questions." Professor Eric Werner, the editor of a new song book for youngsters, just told me that he planned to reprint two or more of Jessie Sampter's poems in the collection. This is a sort of immortality, which, while it does not preserve the whole stature of Jessie Sampter, the fighter and the singer, would, nonetheless, have been highly appreciated by her.

A "living" memorial of Jessie's life and work is in existence in Israel: it is the Rest Home, *Bet Yesha,* as they called it after Jessie's death, which has become one of the beauty spots of modern Israel. At the time of its foundation, there were twelve beds at the Rest Home; now there are one hundred. During all the years since her death, a devoted staff of workers, boys and girls, have been anxious to develop the Home and improve its living conditions.

The Rest Home, according to the administration, was purely vegetarian until the Israeli War of Liberation. At that time, most of its visitors were wounded soldiers, and, in compliance with the military physicians' request, they had to introduce fish dishes. "A few months ago, the administration was compelled to introduce meat as well. Because of the food situation in Israel, most people were not prepared to come to a vegetarian Rest Home and many reservations were cancelled. So they had to start giving meat dishes to those who asked for them."

Of course, Jessie Sampter, as author of the eloquent essay, "Vegetarians in Palestine" would have been startled by this development. She was happy that the "Rest Home, a living experiment in vegetarianism, satisfied both its founders and its guests." But she would not have been surprised at the administration's conceding meat dishes out of considerations of economy and competition. For what was to her the main thing remained — to provide a chance of recuperation and relaxation to "teachers and workers" who could not pay high prices.

"The happy household where differences of class, nationality and education are subordinated to the interests of the group assembled and to the pleasures of art and nature," as Jessie wrote in her essay, is still there; in the management of the Rest Home there are still *haverot* who worked there during the lifetime of Yesha, and they make every effort to continue the work in her spirit. Last, not least, the garden is still there, with its eucalyptus grove, where Yesha established her "work room" and with its flowers, whose seeds she got from America and which she planted to serve as a living bond between her native land and her new home in Israel.

But while "Yesha" has become a saga in Israel, and Jessie Sampter is a familiar name to the authors and readers of Jewish Reform prayer books in America, we ought not to overlook the fact that Jessie Sampter's religious message has not been fulfilled to this day. And this very fact makes her words more timely. Perhaps the Jewish People, fortified by the newborn State of Israel, may well be on the threshold of realizing her visions. About thirty years ago, she wrote in her autobiography, *The Speaking Heart*:

> "I am writing for a new Law springing from the life of my people — from my own life. . . .
> "I want to gather the spirit of our hopeful past for the building of our future. Our young Pioneers shall create the new living Law. I, too, am a Pioneer; if not young in years, I fulfill my youth in the folk youth of my rejuvenated people. . . ."

This renovation and acceptance of our Jewish law, which Jessie Sampter had waited for ever since she set foot on the soil of Palestine, has been called the "next great step, which has to be taken by the Free Jewish people." The free and sovereign people of Israel have it once again in their hands to take up the work of an Ezra and a Hillel. "Not only the people, but the law of Israel must live." This was what Jessie Sampter had been waiting for throughout her life. It is as needful today as it was when she died fifteen years ago. May her lifelong dream find fulfillment — "now, soon in our days," and in the days of the reborn State of Israel! Only then will Jessie Sampter's prophetic message be fulfilled.

In Givat Brenner, our question "Is Yesha alive today?" will certainly be answered in the affirmative. Perhaps a day will come, when, peace having returned to Israel, the grateful *haverim* and *haverot* of Givat Brenner will erect in the garden of the Rest Home, where Jessie loved to work and dream, a monument to Jessie Sampter, harbinger of peace.

APPENDIX A

TWO CHILDHOOD POEMS*

The Old Coat

(July, 1898)

An old gray coat, a tattered rag, of yore
Worth ten good English pounds of gold or more
But where, through silent years of slow decay,
A vile intrusive life hath found its way;
To-day I spied it, in a single breath
I put the whole community to death.

An old gray earth where every year anew
Old trees seem young, and withered hearts seem true;
A nest of men, who daily multiply,
Who live and suffer, and in suffering, die,
Have gathered there, and making all their own,
Have lived and perished thus from times unknown.

Some day, mayhap, a mighty storm will sweep
Across the earth, with murmurs dread and deep,
And hurl away the musty haunts of men
And never shall a trace be seen again.
So all the labor and the patient pain
And all the waiting shall have been in vain?

An old gray coat, a garment long laid by;
Yet in its folds my hopes were wont to die.

* See Chapter I, p. 14.

An old gray earth, a weary earth where life
Hath labored, loved and perished in its strife.
Still, Nature destined to a better goal
The mighty efforts of the human soul.

From *Hester Lynn*

My School

Oh you have bonny things to tell of school-days long gone by
Your cheeks were ruddy as you went, your hearts were
      light — but I
I watched you caper down the road to knowledgeland —
      and then,
With smiles to keep the tears away, I wandered toward the
      glen,
The woods, the rills, the haunted nooks where many an
      imp and elf
Was waiting for the sickly child, my poor untutored self.

2.

I lay upon the balmy earth, a canopy of pine
Was spread above to cool my brow, a kingly court was mine,
Where music swelled for freedom's sake, and asked for
      nothing more,
While venerable teachers came to teach me ancient lore.
I fear their pupil was not apt, and yet I nothing doubt,
But all the masters of the world were gathered thereabout.

3.

The rill was whispering 'mid the ferns, enchanted as a dream
It hastened down and lost itself within the wider stream,

It told me of a mighty world that never thought of me,
And myriad little lab'ring brooks that perish in the sea.
And all unheeded by my side I saw a lily spring,
It taught me of the Love and Law that guideth everything.

4.

From out the throats of wondrous birds melodious anthems
    poured
Of all the lovely, holy things that live not for reward,
And when upon the liquid sky the rose of even smiled,
I turned me slowly home again, a solemn, dreaming child.
Your books were lightly thrown aside, you bubbled o'er
    with play,
But I was pondering o'er the things I learned in school that
    day.

From: *St. Nicholas Magazine* . . .

APPENDIX B

JESSIE E. SAMPTER'S TESTIMONY ON THE 1929 ARAB RIOTS

It is a sacred duty to use this opportunity of writing freely of the events of the last ten days in Palestine and sending my testimony with a personal messenger, an American citizen who is sailing from here. All mails are censored. But indignation and horror and mental and emotional exhaustion are almost as great a barrier against words.

The American citizens in Jewish Palestine sent a cable to Washington asking the Government to protest against the criminal negligence of the local administration which, among other horrors, was responsible for the piecemeal butchery — to be precise — of eight American boys, defenseless students in the Academy of Hebron. Although I contributed a word or two to the cable, I was not able to sign it because I am no longer an American citizen but a Palestinian. Never was I so glad as now of this change of citizenship. I have a right in the protection of my own government in my own country and I do not want to be tempted to ask for special privileges.

Ten minutes ago I spoke with one of the American students who escaped whole from the butchery at Hebron. He is sailing to the States in two weeks to visit his parents and show himself alive, to bear testimony, and then when the Yeshiva in Hebron is restored, to return there to continue his studies. He is a tall pale boy, deathly pale after his return from the dead, very gentle and quiet and unhysterical in his manner and weirdly objective in his talk. When he came to visit us this morning, he made for the piano as a tired runner would for a soda fountain, and he played from memory Liszt's

Liebestraum. Then, standing there by the piano, I asked him if he would tell me, and I told him why, and he came away to talk to us.

Three weeks before the outbreak, students at the Academy received letters from Russia and Poland begging them to return home, because rumor had it that the Communist party in London was conniving with the Arabs to effect a general massacre of the Jews. Days before the attack, the air was electric with emotions released by the assaults on Jews by Arabs in Jerusalem and the jocularly mild reproaches by the British administration. The young men of the Yeshivah visited the governor of Hebron to ask for protection. To be exact, the Vice-governor; the English governor of the district had gone on his vacation and had appointed a Christian Arab in his stead. The governor assured the boys that there was no danger, that they could go home and be quiet, *that he would be responsible for anything that happened.* As the threats increased and they tried to reach him again, they were refused admittance; they were told that he was out of town, a bald lie, and they were not permitted the door. On Friday there was an attack in Hebron. A Jew was killed and several were wounded. The students demanded that the Jewish community be afforded the protection of the prison; in Hebron there are only about 550 Jews among a population of about 20,000 Moslem Arabs. (It is a center of fanaticism from ancient times, one of the few places where, for this reason, the Jews have never penetrated in large numbers. It is very beautiful and fertile country.) The request for asylum in the prison was refused.

On Friday — that was August 23, — several automobiles full of armed Arabs drove from Hebron to Jerusalem to make trouble. The British authorities did not permit them to enter the city and turned them back upon Hebron, without relieving them of their arms or warning them or hindering them in

the least. Neither did they receive an escort to chaperone
them. On Saturday at 11 o'clock before noon there burst
upon all Jewish Hebron a wild orgy of murder. The students
were housed in two dormitories, one with over 40, the other
with only 13 lodgers. The larger house was sacked and the
unarmed young men were chopped to pieces with stilettoes,
hatchets, knives and a club resembling a tomahawk; few shots
were fired. As the smaller house was about to be tackled, the
Arab landlord rode in hastily from his vineyard and placed
himself in the doorway and so protected them with his own
body. From behind broken windows the crouching boys
peeped down and witnessed what it is quite unnecessary to
describe. The peculiar type of barbarity used consisted in
beginning at the fingers to cut up the victim. Most of the
boys in the big house were murdered and practically all who
escaped were maimed. The toll of dead was about sixty-one.
Later, when the Government decided to act, 13 Arabs were
shot. Reliable witnesses told my informant that in the city
Arab police helped with the butchery in the heat of action.
That is nothing new here.

The wounded were taken to the Government hospital. The
living were taken to prison for their protection at 2 o'clock.
There 485 refugees were crowded into a few rooms, and ten
loaves of Arab bread were distributed among them, until on
Monday the women and children were taken to Jerusalem.
Some money was borrowed from the wardens to procure quite
inadequate food. There was no place to lie down, there were
no sanitary arrangements, and the only water to be had was
cistern water and not fit to drink — "not fit to drink for
a dog" added my informant. The refugees were treated like
prisoners, shouted at, pushed and beaten back, when they at-
tempted to go to the office to state their demands. The men
were kept there four days.

I am sitting on the veranda of a home in the northern outskirts of Tel Aviv, facing the Mediterranean. Out there silhouetted softly against the mother-of-pearl sky stands a hard British battleship, telling me that now I am safe, at least at long range. As I sat there, wondering how I could go on writing at all, the postman brought me a letter from Jerusalem. It is easiest to copy it:

> This horrible fact is a fact: The British Government was incapable or did not want to protect us from the wild hordes, which could have been done quite easily. In every place that protection was given lives have been saved. If not for our boys who have been prepared since last week, Jerusalem would have been worse than Hebron, and Hebron is so horrible that I cannot describe it. The wounded that have been brought here are so terribly wounded, cut off fingers and arms. Mrs. H.'s sons (Americans) are simply mutilated. I cannot yet speak of it. I and my family, we are alive, but the heart is bleeding. And if this was necessary, we will, of course, accept it, but it is very hard.

To any historically minded person — that is — any one who recognizes that present events form part of the historic stream and, knowing the contours, can approximately fortell the course of the flow — the first act of the present tragi-farce was staged last Yom Kippur, ten months ago, and the last act with its triumphal procession and its glorious promises, is still to come. In our serious business, such side-shows for the amusement of colonial employees should be sternly forbidden. It is hard for me, without legal training, to undertake an argument on the legal rights involved in the "Wailing Wall dispute." . . . The Wailing Wall, as a religious relic in the Arab sense, is not worth one Jewish life . . . As a national symbol it is as dangerous as all banners, slogans and catch words. . . .

My own personal experiences have been comparatively mild. I happened to be away from home in this outskirt of Tel Aviv for a summer holiday. We were threatened with attack; we were copiously guarded by our own boys.